Praise for *Downs...*

"In the tradition of Studs Terkel's *Working, Downshifting* is brilliant journalism; journalism with substance and scope—the best. Saltzman offers a fascinating picture of work today, taking on the central myth of our age—the myth of work-for-itself as the unquestioned center of existence—and describes a striking new phenomenon."

—Benjamin Hunnicutt, Professor,
Department of Leisure Studies, University of Iowa,
and author of *Work Without End*

"Amy Saltzman's book really struck a note with me and Rosalynn. Even during intensely competitive years in business, while campaigning, and in public office, we tried to relax and carve out family time. *Downshifting* is a guide to sane career planning, and will help remove the guilt feelings from enjoying life."

—Former President Jimmy Carter

"Amy Saltzman gives us examples of people who did something courageous and imaginative to solve their problems. Happily, *Downshifting* offers no charts or magic formulas and few generalizations. It is good journalism. It features well-written profiles of interesting, sympathetic people who found a better balance in a world where there is never enough time."

—*Baltimore Sun*

"Amy Saltzman's book could not be more timely. It provides a viable new definition of career success as well as alternative models of advancement that will help professionals free themselves from what is fast becoming a prison of work."

—Suzanne Gordon, author of *Prisoners of Men's Dreams*

DOWN-SHIFTING

REINVENTING SUCCESS
ON A SLOWER TRACK

AMY SALTZMAN

HarperPerennial
A Division of HarperCollins*Publishers*

A hardcover edition of this book was published in 1991 by HarperCollins Publishers.

DOWNSHIFTING. Copyright © 1991 by Amy Saltzman. All rights reserved. Printed in the United States of America. No part of this book may be used or reproduced in any manner whatsoever without written permission except in the case of brief quotations embodied in critical articles and reviews. For information address HarperCollins Publishers, Inc., 10 East 53rd Street, New York, NY 10022.

HarperCollins books may be purchased for educational, business, or sales promotional use. For information, please call or write: Special Markets Department, HarperCollins Publishers, Inc., 10 East 53rd Street, New York, NY 10022. Telephone: (212) 207-7528; Fax: (212) 207-7222.

First HarperPerennial edition published 1992.

Designed by Cassandra J. Pappas

The Library of Congress has catalogued the hardcover edition as follows:

Saltzman, Amy, 1958–
    Downshifting : reinventing on a slower track / by Amy
Saltzman.
    p. cm.
    Includes bibliographical references and index.
    ISBN 0-06-016579-0
    1. Career development—United States—Public opinion.
2. Professional employees—United States—Attitudes. 3. Public
opinion—United States. 4. Professional employees—United States—
Time management. I. Title.
HF5381.S257   1991
658.4′093′0973—dc20   90-55552

ISBN 0-06-092158-7 (pbk.)

92 93 94 95 96 CC/HC 10 9 8 7 6 5 4 3 2 1

To my parents,
Paul and Bettylu Saltzman

Contents

Acknowledgments

This book could not have been completed without the help and support of my family, friends and colleagues. My editor Janet Goldstein's enthusiasm for the project was infectious. Her clear-sighted vision and guidance fueled the book from its bare-bones beginnings to the final manuscript. My agent, Kristine Dahl, also provided crucial direction and support, particularly during the difficult early stages of the writing process.

In the research phase, dozens of people provided their time and resources. A special thanks to Janice Benjamin and Linda Marks.

My friends at *U.S. News & World Report* offered valuable advice and were a constant source of reassurance. I am especially grateful to Avery Comarow for giving me the time to work on the project.

Finally, I want to thank Steve Wellner, for his patience, love and great cooking.

DOWNSHIFTING

1

The Solitude of Empty Porches

On a warm, cloudless Saturday in November, the massive Victorian homes of Newark Street look like the elegant, ghostly façades of an old Hollywood set. One dramatic four-story structure, with its darkened windows and series of intricate wraparound porches, could be the backdrop for an epic tale of southern love and romance. A few houses down, a yellow clapboard home trimmed in white has the studied country casualness of one of those glossy Ralph Lauren ads. On the large front porch, a white wicker rocking chair appears to have been angled precisely to capture the soft shadow of an ancient elm. An arrangement of miniature brown and gold Indian corn dangles above a brass door knocker. A multicolored oval rag rug sprawled across the porch serves as a massive welcome mat.

Newark Street has always been something of an icon for Washington, D.C., professionals, a fantasy of idealized urban living. Its carefully stylized homes are painted perfect shades of gray, yellow and blue. Its gracious romantic porches are tailor-made for reading Faulkner, chatting with the neighbors, watching the world go by. Winding like a lonely river off busy Connecticut Avenue, a few blocks from the Cleveland Park Metro station, Newark Street is conveniently located in the heart of northwest Washington. It is a realtor's dream, with homes that typically sell for upwards of $1 million.

About halfway through writing this book, I happened to take a stroll along Newark Street. As always, I was impressed by its beauty. It was an unseasonably mild fall day, too mild for even a sweater. I made my way slowly up the narrow sidewalks, gawking enviously at those magnificent homes. Ten minutes into my walk, a man of about thirty-five, wearing tan slacks and a white Oxford shirt, with a leather portfolio tucked under one arm, emerged from the Ralph Lauren lookalike home. He stood for a minute on the porch, sucked in the warm air and made a beeline for his light gold Acura Legend. At first glance, there was nothing especially extraordinary about the scene. But for reasons that weren't immediately clear, the image of the man on the porch continued to nag at me for the next several days. A few weeks later, as I was sitting down to another day of piecing together the stacks of interviews and notes that would become this book, I started to understand why. In all the times I had walked down Newark Street, I had never once seen anyone sitting on even one of those picture-perfect porches.

As I continued writing, the image of those beautiful, empty million-dollar façades stuck with me. In one neat snapshot, they said it all.

Emptiness in the midst of luxury, wealth in the midst of despair

As the 1980s drew to a close, there was much talk in the media about how the extravagances of the Reagan era were now behind us. It was time, it seemed, to move on. "The Decade of Excess," screamed a front-page story in *USA Today,* was over. Our over-worked, overburdened lives were beating us into the ground. Physically and mentally we were starting to pay a heavy price. The nineties, the article promised, would emerge as a decade when "people began to care."

In the midst of the loud headlines, one could only wonder when all this would start to happen and how exactly we would get from here to there. Would our values as a society undergo a collective shift as the bells rang in a new decade? With the lessons of fallen Wall Street tycoons and a skittish stock market behind us, would we all at once realize that our striving for material and professional gain had left us without lives or a sense of belonging to something larger than ourselves? Would we then, in unison, come up with a workable alternative?

The problem was and continues to be an absence of clear alternatives for change. When it comes to defining a successful life in American society, today's career professionals seem stuck between two ultimately dissatisfying extremes: dropping out completely and creating their own vision of a better world, or working within the system and speeding up their pace on the success treadmill. Even as we search for ways to change our lives, we seem to lack the tools to create a new success imagery that would provide us with options beyond these extremes. In-stead, we have allowed our professional identities to define us and control us. We have looked to outside forces such as the corporation, the university and the media to provide us with a script for leading satisfying, worthwhile and successful lives.

This book is aimed at those of us who have dutifully played the part of career professional to the exclusion, in some cases, of almost everything else that gives life purpose and meaning. And it is aimed at those of us who have struggled to lessen the commitment of time and self required to maintain a successful career, but who still find themselves running the same race day in and day out. As career professionals in the 1990s we come equipped with a unique set of societal and personal expectations. We implicitly believe that work should serve a purpose in our lives beyond allowing us to put food on the table and meet the monthly mortgage payment. As business executives, corporate attorneys or professional writers, we don't punch a time clock or look to others to provide us with the motivation and incentive to get the job done. We want to work hard and achieve recognition in our careers because, for us, professional success is an inherently satisfying and worthwhile goal. It is also the clearest measure of a successful life.

What is also central to the mindset of this group, as I will define it in the following pages, is a tendency to set goals and measure success along a vertical career path that we have come to describe as the "career ladder" or the "fast track." One is not successful, according to this school of thought, unless one is consistently moving up the ladder in some clearly quantifiable way. You'll know you are truly successful, writes Michael Korda in *Success!,* when "you've gone that one step further in wealth, fame or achievement, than you ever dreamed was possible." [1] The career professional in our society today represents a comfortable standard, or "social norm," as Barbara Ehrenreich puts it in *Fear of Falling,* her study of the "professional middle class," to which everyone else can aspire. [2] But what the career climber has also come to represent in recent years is the dissatisfaction that results from striving too hard to achieve an extremely narrow set of goals.

Over the past few years, as I have conducted my own extensive interviews with professionals across the country, the yearning for change has become more pronounced. While the fast track and its accompanying imagery of career achievement still has its appeal, there is a pervasive feeling that we have drastically overemphasized its importance; that as individuals and as a society we need to reinvent our notion of success.

Among the many telling indicators of this in recent years has been the apparent willingness of professionals to slow down their career advancement in order to spend more time with their families. In a 1989 survey of 1,000 men and women conducted by Robert Half International, Inc., 82 percent of the women and 78 percent of the men said they would choose a career path with flexible full-time work hours and more family time, but slower career advancement, over one with inflexible work hours and faster career advancement. Two out of three of the men and women surveyed said they would be willing to reduce their work hours and salaries by an average of 13 percent in order to have more family and personal time, and just one-third said they would be likely to accept a promotion if it required them to spend less time with their families. In another poll—this one conducted by the Roper Organization in 1990—for the first time in fifteen years respondents said leisure (41 percent), rather than work (36 percent), was "the important thing" in their lives in response to a question posed annually. In 1985, work came out ahead of leisure by a score of 46 percent to 33 percent.

Such shifting attitudes are in part a reaction to practical realities, most notably the emergence over the past decade of the two-career family. But the numbers also reflect something deeper. There is a sense that as a nation we have been operating in remote control, obediently going through the correct motions but somehow missing the point. By the end of the 1980s, there was a growing realization by exhausted superwomen and supermen that their successful lives lacked substance. As one New York woman, a publishing consultant, told me: "There are days when you feel like you've mastered it all—the job, the family, your romantic life; that you've finally got it right. But then, just as your head hits the pillow after another exhausting day, it occurs to you that all you've really mastered is your super-efficient schedule. There is this feeling of striving and striving but never really improving yourself."

Then why keep striving? Economic factors are the most obvious reasons. Yet most of the people I interviewed for this book had surpassed middle-class lifestyles. In fact, in terms of income, the "professional middle class" is actually more of an upper middle class, an economic and successful elite which, Barbara Ehrenreich calculates, represents no more than 20 percent of the population. [3] Those I spoke with had incomes ranging from about $30,000 for academics and writers to more than $200,000 for big-city lawyers, doctors, corporate vice-presidents and television journalists. Almost everyone earned enough to own a home, pay for the children's college education and afford such extras as vacations, health club memberships, therapy and a range of enlightening cultural activities.

Although many admitted that their incomes had far outpaced their "needs," they typically spoke of being "trapped" by the lifestyles that their big raises and bonuses had bought them. "The more successful we were, the more money it seemed we needed just to stay on top of the mortgage payments and maintain our expensive offices," recalls family therapist and writer Claudia Bepko, who with her partner Jo-Ann Krestan recently moved from an affluent New Jersey suburb to set up a practice in Brunswick, Maine. The two women opted to make a shift in their careers and lifestyles when they found their professional victories overwhelming their personal needs. "It was hard to see the point of being successful if all it gave us was more work and less time to do the things we really wanted to do," says Bepko.

Even those I spoke with who were still working to make ends meet generally admitted that it was not the money that motivated them. It was the challenge of "being their best," although most conceded that they were living anything but full or deep lives. It was as if they were repeating a kind of mantra, a pledge to the good life reinforced day in and day out by sparkling media images of modern-day success. Consider this television commercial for a major airline: A dressed-for-success mom leaves her toddler at the day care center, flies to New York City, gives a boardroom presentation, eats a power lunch, and makes it back before nightfall to pick up her daughter, not a hair out of place or an emotion unhinged. It is worth noting that this spot ran in 1989, the same year the Half survey was released and several years after the superwoman was first dismissed in major magazine articles and popular books as an absurd, even dangerous, concept.

Consciously or not, however, we continue to incorporate such images into our everyday lives. After all, as we look around our own offices, those who have risen highest often seem to have that same glamorous, on-top-of-it-all façade. We may suspect that everything is not as rosy as it appears, but after so many years of being told this is success, we now feel resolved to hold on to it. The image of the super-successful fast-tracker who manages to "do it all" has always been hard to resist. It offers an appealing challenge: mastery over modern-day madness, total control, perfection. It's no wonder that without any obvious alternatives, and with so little time to reflect on where our hectic lives are taking us, we prepare ourselves each day to tackle the same increasingly empty role.

The cult of busyness

Barreling her way down Madison Avenue, a large black bag weighing down one shoulder and a shiny reptile-skinned Filofax pressed against her chest like a newborn baby, my friend looked as if she had just emerged from one of those breathless fast-tracker commercials. From a distance she had that look of the eighties: hurried, determined, I've-got-somewhere-to-go-and-I'm-going-to-get-there-quickly self-confidence. As we moved closer to each other, however, and she came into clearer focus, the image seemed to lose its neat, glossy edges. In her haste to get wherever she was going, she had buttoned her black wool coat so that one side hung lower than the other; her mustard-colored cashmere scarf was untied and in danger of slipping off her shoulder; small pastel slips of paper overflowed from her Filofax notebook. The uniform was right—all the pieces were there—but the overall picture was slightly off-center.

It was the winter of 1987, about six months before I moved to Washington, D.C., and both my friend and I were working as editors for New York–based monthly magazines. We had been trying to get together for months. A few phone calls had been exchanged, with promises of drinks or dinner, but nothing had materialized. On this particular occasion, we had barely said hello when my friend announced that she was running late for an appointment. She assumed her "gotta run, I'll call you, we'll do lunch" pose as she breathlessly asked me how I was doing. I told her that things were fine, work was interesting, although I wasn't allowing it to take over my life; I was doing volunteer work a few evenings a week, reading a lot and working on a short story that I didn't think would ever get published but was enjoying anyway.

She seemed baffled. "That's really nice," she said, apparently unable to grasp the idea that I wasn't particularly busy at work—and was enjoying it. The fact was, I had made a conscious decision to take life a little slower. I had recently gone through a divorce and was feeling a need to reconnect with areas and relationships outside of work. In fact, I had purposely not gone after a promotion because I knew the job would eat up too many evenings and weekends. Besides, while it might have looked impressive, I wasn't sure the position suited me at that point in my life. The decision, however, had not been made lightly and had continued to nag at me. When I saw my friend, I realized why. If we weren't always moving ahead and aiming for something higher and more impressive, if we didn't have that look of constantly being busy and in motion, we were somehow boring or even losers.

The fact was, my life felt fuller, more interesting and more worthwhile than I could ever remember: I was having long dinners with friends and making a point of going to the theater regularly for the first time since moving to New York nearly four years before. I had even spent a large chunk of a recent rainy Sunday afternoon talking on the phone with my grandmother in Omaha, discovering for the first time that underneath her faltering speech and advancing years she was an interesting and perceptive woman with a fascinating past. Although I was happy and relaxed and thoroughly enjoying myself, my life didn't fall into any neat, easily packaged definition of success in our culture. I couldn't explain it in a 30-second sound bite, not enough at least to satisfy an old friend racing to an appointment on Madison Avenue.

Much of the initial thinking behind this book was set in motion during the period of that encounter three years ago. I was a senior editor of *Success* magazine at the time, enjoying the intellectual and creative challenges of helping a young publication take hold in a competitive field. But I found myself feeling increasingly ill at ease with the message of a magazine that typically defined success in narrow, self-interested terms. It was a message that those of us on the staff struggled with almost daily and tried to resolve, for the short term at least, with occasional profiles of do-gooders. But the overall tone of the publication, like others in the business magazine field, remained one of hyped-up, aggressive success. War and sports metaphors appeared in nearly every issue. The theme was "go for it." And do it quickly.

The chance meeting with my friend that day solidified my misgivings. I realized that our success culture could no longer be rationalized as just one part of our lives—namely, our work—but that it permeated everything. The cult of busyness was more than mere media hype. It was the new badge of professionalism and had seeped into nearly every facet of our rushed existences. Even our leisure had developed a hurried quality. The "gotta run, I'll call you, we'll do lunch" expression wasn't just another yuppie stereotype. It reflected an attitude about even the most basic and uncomplicated forms of leisure. The simple pleasure of having lunch with a friend had taken on the characteristics of work. It had become programmed and scheduled.

In frenzied offices, on bumper-to-bumper freeways and on busy downtown streets, there has been a pervasive feeling that something is amiss; that it is all getting out of hand. This sense of impending chaos has been reinforced by opinion polls and national surveys suggesting that we are spending more time working and less time playing than during any period in recent history. According to a 1988 Louis Harris poll, the average American work week jumped from under 41 hours to almost 47 hours between 1973 and 1988; for professionals it soared to 52 hours. Leisure time, during that same period, also took a beating: it shrunk by 37 percent. We had less time for romance, for hobbies, for vacations. In 1988, the average time spent away from home on holiday was 4.8 nights, down from 6.0 in 1985, according to the U.S. Travel Data Service. In a 1987 study, Marriott Corporation found that trips of three days or less accounted for 73 percent of vacations taken by those surveyed.

Sociologists and pollsters continue to debate whether Americans as a whole actually have less time or merely feel they do. The fact is, leisure today has something of a negative connotation. Having too much leisure implies we are wasting time and not working hard enough to get ahead. With so little time and so much of it devoted to professional pursuits, spending a Saturday afternoon on the front porch reading a book, talking to the neighbors or writing a letter to a friend is out of the question. Leisure is instead one more neatly packaged item on the good life itinerary, reserved for a week at an executive spa retreat or a ski holiday in the Colorado Rockies.

In many ways it has always been easier to act as if there were no options; as if we didn't have a choice. Accepting the standard definition of work success frees us from experiencing any existential angst about what to do with our lives. "The idea of decreasing work is hair-raising for many people," says Benjamin Kline Hunnicutt, a professor of leisure studies at the University of Iowa and author of *Work Without End,* a study of America's growing work culture in the years following the Depression. "If we worked less we would suddenly be confronted with the problem of freedom and what to do with it. Work is an escape from freedom." But in allowing us to avoid the possibilities offered by freedom, the fast track shackles us to a set of standards and rules that prohibit us from leading truly successful, happy lives.

Images of control: the fast-tracker versus the dropout

Click.

A young executive is confiding to a colleague that he thinks he may have blown it. The phone system he painstakingly researched and bought for the company has turned out to be obsolete. "You don't think they're going to boot me out of here—over a phone system?" he asks nervously. His friend, who clearly has his eye on the next rung of the career ladder, is superficially comforting: "Don't be ridiculous. Relax, John." But it is painfully clear that John had better start updating his resume. He should have chosen AT&T.

Click . . . click.

The "thirtysomething" executive is about to realize his dream.

"Hoffman," says his firm's elderly managing partner, "you started as a junior in the mailroom . . . and now we're making you a senior partner . . . That means giving up that piddly teenage sports car."

Hoffman: "No problem."

Managing partner: "Disposing of that adolescent Village loft."

Hoffman: "No problem."

Managing partner: "And absolutely, positively no more of those childish Frosted Flakes."

With that, young Hoffman marches back to his lowly job in the mailroom, where he is free to chow down on a sumptuous bowl of his favorite sugary cereal.

While fiddling with the remote control one evening, these

two distinct images of our success culture flashed on my television screen. In both commercials, the underlying theme is control. The cereal commercial suggests that the only way to win is, in essence, to give up and live your life outside an impossible, overly controlling system. The AT&T spot, on the other hand, reinforces our insecurities and sense of being out of control by suggesting that if we don't get our act together and do whatever it takes to please the boss, the window of opportunity will slam shut and we will be left out in the cold. Despite their vastly different tones and styles, the two commercials hit at similar feelings of frustration and fear that force us, often against our better instincts, to mold ourselves to a rigid career track.

These two commercials also represent what many of us have come to view as our only real choice: to keep pushing harder and running faster along a preordained fast track or to drop out completely. We play out a mental dance between these two extremes, typically fantasizing about the latter as we immerse ourselves in the former. The fast-tracker and the dropout are easily definable roles. They don't require any lengthy explanations, like the one I felt compelled to give my friend on Madison Avenue. But as roles we force ourselves to play they are inherently limiting and ultimately unsatisfying.

Explicitly or implicitly, the underlying assumptions about success in many modern professions reinforce the fast-track archetype. While in law school at the University of California at Berkeley, Brad Lewis had it pounded into him that success in his field meant "going to work for a prestigious law firm, billing a lot of hours and making it to partner as quickly as possible." Lewis dutifully followed the roadmap laid out for him, accepting a job as an associate for a highly regarded Los Angeles firm, regularly working evenings and weekends, and becoming increasingly unhappy with the options available to him on the legal fast track. When he started to think about making a switch to a job with the

U.S. Attorney's office—a position he felt better suited to both personally and professionally—the image of himself as a high-paid partner for a big-city firm stood in the way. "I was worried that doing anything different would hinder my career, that people wouldn't consider me as successful just because I wasn't at a top firm, making a lot of money and following the partnership track," says Lewis, who after several months of agonizing took a 40 percent pay cut and made the shift to the U.S. Attorney's office in Sacramento.

The professionals I spoke with, like Lewis, frequently expressed a feeling of being taken over and controlled by success. Many conceded that even as their achievements on the job were pushing them into areas they didn't want to be, they felt compelled to put in longer hours and work harder for the next promotion. The result was that the more successful they became, the further they drifted from the kind of lives they really wanted to lead. "In a funny way, I feel less control over my life now than I ever did before," said Richard Pinto, vice-president of operations for Marriott Residence Inns, based in Sunnyvale, California. At the time I interviewed Pinto, he was spending most of his week on the road traveling to distant properties throughout the western half of the country, leaving him little time to enjoy his California lifestyle and six-figure income or to do the kind of work he liked most—managing hotels.

After his company was taken over by Marriott in 1987, Pinto felt he had no choice but to play the corporate game, which meant accepting promotions he didn't particularly want. "I just felt I was in a position where it would have been impossible to say no. The money wasn't a big thing—I wasn't motivated to have more money. But it just seemed to be inexorable the way things were going." Pinto's complaint is a common one among executives whose positions have been spared after a corporate merger, takeover or downsizing. When the corporate culture itself is permeated with so much uncertainty and insecurity, it seems impossible to ease back and set one's own limits.

It is just such scenarios that frequently lead to burnout and often push professionals toward the other extreme—dropping out. For dropouts, simply pulling back is unfathomable. The world would view them as failures. Their own egos could never endure the beating. But if they drop out completely, if they trade one idealized role for another, and forgo the fast track altogether, they have merely made a "lifestyle choice." Says Edith Gilson: "I worked so hard to get where I was, I couldn't imagine just pulling back. I felt I needed to make a total break."

So after too many years of working 14-hour days, the former senior vice-president of J. Walter Thompson Advertising in New York sold her Manhattan co-op, left behind a vast network of friends and colleagues and moved to the Massachusetts Berkshires. With the money from the sale of her co-op, she opened up a furniture store specializing in new and antique pieces from her native Bavaria. She watched the sun set each day, took long walks in the country, saw deer scamper through her yard, and grew increasingly depressed.

"I had given up this tremendous support system in New York and felt very lonely. For a while I was in a pretty severe depression. It was a time when I was first starting up my business and things weren't always selling. It felt like rejection. I hadn't prepared myself enough beforehand for what it would really be like." Forsaking a successful career for the romance of a simpler country life has long been glamorized in books and movies. In the 1980s, it ironically became one more idealized step on the fast track—a reward for those clever and self-confident enough to buck the system and create their own versions of the good life. What was inevitably missing from the picture, however, was reality. After moving to the Berkshires, Gilson met dozens of other ex-New Yorkers like herself who failed to foresee the emotional and practical complications of chucking it all. Says Gilson, "They gave up their lives and their careers and ended up experiencing a real sense of loss."

For Gilson, the initial act of dropping out gave her the illusion of control. The immediate feeling was one of triumph and freedom. But escape is ultimately a form of self-delusion. As Gilson found: "This isn't a movie role. It's real life."

The challenge of setting limits

Early on in my career, I worked in an office with a man who truly amazed me. Every evening at 5:30, he would flick off the fluorescent light on his dark wood desk, tuck a newspaper under his arm and head out the door, while the rest of us pounded away at our keyboards and made last-minute calls for the next hour or two. He was a star writer for a growing publication. But he never worked evenings or weekends and spoke with equal degrees of excitement about his work and his family. He was no loafer or lazy underachiever. To the contrary. He loved his work, found it inherently engrossing and worthwhile but rarely seemed to worry about where it was going to get him in the corporate hierarchy. His trip up the career ladder had been slower and less dramatic than that of his more aggressive counterparts. But by age 37 he held an impressive and challenging job, and there was little doubt that he would continue to advance at his own, measured pace.

I think about him often when I find myself not having time to return a friend's phone call or take a 20-minute walk during my lunch hour or sit in front of the fire on a chilly winter evening with a good book. I think about him during those "crisis" periods when my competitive instincts and career ambitions seem to be controlling me; when turning down an assignment feels impossible, even though I am already loaded down with more than I can reasonably handle.

Back then, many of us dismissed him as merely brilliant, a remarkable exception to an intractable rule which seemed to be that success only came through personal sacrifice and exhaustion. Looking back, however, it is clear to me that his secret to leading a well-balanced life wasn't superior time-management skills or even talent. It was his ability to utter that word most of us have so much trouble with: "No." What he did, he did exceptionally well. But he was always establishing limits. He took on as much work as he could handle, but when another assignment would have endangered his ability to maintain control over his career and his life, he simply turned it down. Because he was able to focus so well on the work at hand, and inevitably do a superior job at it, no one could complain when he bowed out of the next assignment. His editors never questioned him because he had established a pattern of behavior early on that clearly worked for him and the publication. It didn't occur to anyone to insist that he change it.

We live in a society that is inherently opposed to setting limits. We are told to aim higher, be all we can be, conquer any obstacle that stands in our way. Suggesting to our superiors that we can't do something, that we don't have the time, energy or inclination, seems almos. un-American. It is a mindset that characterizes nearly every American business and organization. "There is a kind of unstated policy here that people are supposed to take on more and more work up until the point where they can just barely handle it," says Dick Muise, an electrical engineer and department manager for AT&T Bell Laboratories in Freehold, New Jersey, who didn't start setting his own limits until he reached that breaking point himself.

From the moment we start interviewing for a job, we are

expected to demonstrate that we have a recklessly competitive drive; that we will enthusiastically immerse ourselves in work to the detriment, if necessary, of a healthy personal life. Consider these classified ads from the July 10, 1989, issue of *Adweek* magazine: "FOR SALE: HIGH-STRESS JOB. Be the highest bidder and this glamour job can be yours." "ACCOUNT DOG. Pit bulls only, golden retrievers need not apply . . . " As one woman, a mid-level systems analyst, complained in a letter to *Working Woman* magazine, all her job interviews in recent years seem to have emphasized the overwork, stressful nature of the positions. "In the most recent, I met with four people during the interview process, and each one described the position as having all of the following elements: high stress; no career advancement; 50-hour weeks; unusually competitive work environment; previous incumbent quit or fired because of inability to handle job or to get along with supervisor . . . It's come to the point where I wonder why interviewers think anyone would accept such a position."[4]

Admittedly, saying "no" in such environments isn't easy. "You just don't do it," says Dick Muise. Showing professionals that they can say "no" is one of the most important tasks of the following pages. This is not a self-help guide. It will not provide you with charts and diagrams and strategies for mapping out a happier, more balanced life. What it will do is offer a new set of role models and images for thinking about success in our society. It may not lead you to make a dramatic shift, as many of those you will read about in the next chapters have. What it almost certainly will do, however, is start you thinking about making minor ones, about learning to set limits in the way my former colleague did. You may accomplish nothing more than what Dick Muise finally did when, after another day of unreasonable demands and responsibilities, he finally put his foot down and uttered that word—"no."

During the past two years, Muise's project responsibilities

had quadrupled and his staff had grown from 20 to 80. "I knew they were piling more on me because they liked my work and knew I could get the job done. I was reluctant to take more on, but I never said anything about it," recalls Muise, who during one particularly rigorous six-month stretch worked nearly every weekend as well as evenings on a series of new telecommunication projects. "It got to the point where I was just feeling incredibly drained, like all the energy was being sucked out of me. I was in a crunch mode almost all the time."

Although his superiors had also started to realize that perhaps the system of spreading a few people over several projects was inefficient and counterproductive, Muise knew that if any real change was going to occur, he would have to speak up. When his boss agreed to cut his work load, but insisted that he continue to handle an especially large and demanding project, Muise, for the first time, voiced his concerns. "I told him that it was not my first choice and that I didn't want it. I made it clear that the only condition under which I would agree to take the project was if it could be reviewed after six months and changes made if things weren't working out." To Muise's surprise, his boss was sympathetic. His only criticism was that he hadn't said something sooner. For Muise's part, just speaking up gave him an incredible feeling of liberation. "It wasn't this big secret anymore. I realized I could say what I felt and take control, and still be respected by the organization." After that, when new assignments came up, they were no longer automatically thrown at Muise. He was able to focus on a few important projects and take charge of his life again.

For many of the professionals you will meet on the following pages, the process of learning to take control of their careers started with just such simple but vital actions. In some cases, they turned those first small steps into more dramatic shifts. A few chose to realign their careers by actually moving back a step or two on the professional ladder. Some determined that the only way to achieve true control was to break their corporate ties and set off on their own. Others came to the conclusion that taking charge of their careers would require relocating to an environment where life itself was calmer and less costly—"dropping out, but not too much," as family therapist Jo-Ann Krestan put it. Through their examples, you will start to see how you can set limits within your own career. That may mean nothing more than speaking up the next time your boss schedules a meeting for 5:30 p.m.—15 minutes before you are supposed to pick up your son at the day care center. Or it may mean realizing that you don't have to respond to every memo and take on every extra project to be successful at your job. At the very least, it will mean recognizing that setting limits and taking control of your professional life starts with you—not your employer.

Where now? Breaking away from gender-based success roles

During the past several decades, women have clung to career success as a salvation from what they saw as the emotionally and intellectually stultifying life of the 1950s-era mom. This is especially true of those in the 35- to 45-year-old age range. This group was the first to sit through women's studies courses in college, to literally and figuratively raise a fist for women's liberation and to have the opportunity to put the tenets of modern feminism into practice. For them, making it in a professional world invented and controlled by men was the clearest way to prove their independence and equality.

"Being successful in a profession was my ticket out of the old roles that were pounded into me as a child," says Eleanor

Wachs, a folklorist in Boston in her early 40s. When Wachs was a young girl in Brooklyn the message from her parents was to choose a profession that would give her the flexibility to be a wife and mother first. "Being a schoolteacher was acceptable because you got the summers off to be with your kids," says Wachs, who has never married and has no children. "I have fought that kind of thinking most of my adult life and looked for female role models who were independent and strong and had made it in a man's world." Following a physically and emotionally draining race for a tenured professorship position that she didn't get, however, Wachs began to consider whether she had made the right choice. She started to see that her singular devotion to an academic career had prevented her from seriously considering other options in her field that would allow her the time to build a happy and successful personal life as well.

For women like Wachs, who have struggled to make it to the top, easing back or even going in reverse is essentially a concession that they can't do it all. But moving beyond such assumptions, as we will see in later chapters, is essential if women are to find a workable balance and create a brand of success that emphasizes personal needs as much as professional. By realizing that academia did not provide the only measure of a successful life, Wachs (Chapter 5) was able to realign her professional goals in a less stressful area outside of a university setting that allowed her to achieve a healthier and happier balance between career and personal needs. For Chicago attorney Robin Schirmer (Chapter 6), breaking out of the restricting success imagery that had been pounded into her by her tradition-minded parents, on one hand, and ambitious professional colleagues, on the other, meant setting off on her own and creating a new role. And for public relations executive Carolyn Bodie (Chapter 7), it meant leaving the stress and isolation of her New York lifestyle for the sense of comfort and meaning provided by her extended family in her hometown of Baltimore.

Men must also cut through layers of expectations and assumptions, many of which have dictated the notion of masculine achievement in our culture for decades. When I started researching this book, I knew there were men out there who were looking to make a shift of emphasis. But I assumed that finding them would take some digging. I heard over and over again that this was primarily a "mommy track" issue; that it was almost exclusively women who were demanding changes and searching for alternative paths that would provide them with both rewarding careers and happy family lives. All those assumptions proved to be dead wrong. If anything, in fact, it was the men who were more desperate for answers and who frequently had to take the biggest steps backwards to gain control of their lives again.

It seemed that every person I asked knew a man who had voluntarily pulled back his career. I would go to a party and meet a lawyer who had given up the daily grind and the high pay of life at a big firm for the more predictable hours and balanced lifestyle offered in a government job. I would take a trip across the country and end up sitting on the plane next to the colleague of a man who had demoted himself out of a high-level management job and who himself was considering such a move. My hairdresser, upon learning about the book I was writing, offered one of his male clients as a perfect example.

On the parenting issue alone, it is becoming more evident that men are looking for solutions to the absent father syndrome and, like women, are increasingly torn between work and family. In an AT&T study of employees with children who were under 18 years old, 73 percent of the men said they had dealt with family issues while at work. A national study by Opinion Research Corporation found that male managers under 40 were the least satisfied of any group in the work force with the amount of time their jobs left them for family life. "Young fathers today want to take a radically different approach toward parenting than they remember their fathers taking," says Stanley Rosenberg, a professor of psychiatry at Dartmouth University medical school who is conducting a long-term study of 500 men in the baby boom and previous generation. Egged on by their wives, these men are far more demanding of themselves in the parenting role. "They remember the remote, emotionally distant fifties-era father figure that they grew up with and want no part of it," says Rosenberg.

But many of the men I spoke with were not parents or husbands, and often were too young to be going through a midlife crisis. What they had in common instead was an overwhelming sense that they had given up too much for their careers and that by blindly accepting the standard masculine ideal of achievement, they had pushed themselves into roles that had little to do with who they really were or what they wanted out of their lives. "My true nature was always that of a very loving individual," says Philip Sardella, who gave up a high-level human resources position at Digital Equipment Corporation for a lesser role as an in-house personnel consultant for the company. "But I covered myself with armor because I didn't view those traits as being valuable. I was always playing a role." For men like Sardella, redefining masculine achievement means learning to be honest about what kind of life and work they want for themselves, not living according to the narrow standards laid out by friends, family and society as a whole. When Sardella gave up his top management position to get back to the work he most enjoyed—counselling employees—there were those around him who saw his backward step as a sign of weakness and failure. Not Sardella. "For the first time in my life," he says, "I wasn't playing a role."

In search of a new role model

Career tracks trap us, in large part, by playing into our insecurities. The late Herbert A. Shepard, a career consultant and business professor, wrote that corporate reward systems are "geared to common deficiencies—needs for status, approval, power."

By such a definition, a career consists of doing exactly what is needed to achieve such rewards and move ahead. If that means working 80-hour weeks, having no personal life and not even truly enjoying the work one is doing, then so be it. "In many companies the message about careers is very clear," notes Shepard. "Not only is your career more important than the rest of your life, it is more important than your life."[5]

Taking control of the forces that almost imperceptibly push us along a destructive path—a path that we have learned to call "success"—is the first step toward change. Most of us accept almost blindly the media imagery and corporate ideology that is handed us. We adapt ourselves to a career culture that defines normal, mature adults as those who pursue a traditional career path, achieve a certain amount of material comforts and learn to live with the tradeoffs and compromises that go along with this standard definition of modern life. When we feel in danger of losing our footing, we read another self-help book to learn to manage our time more efficiently, deal with stress more effectively, become corporate players. Rarely do we question the intrinsic value of the career track itself, just our ability to endure its growing demands.

After all, we have had no real role models to show us another way. Quite the opposite, in fact. In the last decade, our role models have glorified the most extreme aspects of the traditional career track. For lack of clear alternatives, we have idolized the absurdly affluent and obnoxiously powerful. Achieving stupendous wealth became the clearest and in many ways the simplest means of reaching that ultimate goal: complete control over our lives.

In the following pages you will meet a new breed of professional, including business managers, engineers, doctors, lawyers, journalists, academics and a host of others. They are not dropouts. They have not given up the intellectual, emotional and financial rewards of professional success but have learned to put limits on it. They embody a practical alternative for rethinking our notion of success from one that glamorizes overwork, overefficiency and exhaustion to one that embraces family, community and one's own needs beyond work.

At first, they may seem unlikely role models. They are career downshifters—people who have taken control of their lives not by continually aiming higher on the career ladder but, in some cases, by moving back a notch or two. They include the plateauer, who has intentionally stayed in place by turning down promotions and other opportunities for typical advancement; the back-tracker, who has bucked the traditional upward track to take a few steps down the ladder within his or her organization or profession; the career shifter, who has found creative and more satisfying uses for his or her talents in a new setting that places less emphasis on a traditional fast track; the self-employer, who has taken control of his or her life by transferring all that training on the fast track to an enterprise where he or she can define the work and set the pace; and the urban escapee, who hasn't sacrificed everything for a romantic fantasy but has found that a successful career can be built outside of costly, stressful urban centers.

The solutions these career downshifters are finding go several steps beyond the short-term remedies offered by corporations. Some have created their own formulas for achieving a fuller and more personal life success. Instead of seeking quick fixes, they have looked inward and learned the importance of setting limits and clarifying needs. Their singular emphasis on progress within a career has been replaced by a broader range of goals encompassing emotional, creative and spiritual achievement.

By holding up a new kind of role model, this book presents an alternative to the long-held notion of career success. More than simply slowing down their careers, the people you will meet in the following chapters have adopted a new attitude about what it means to lead a successful life in our culture. For many, that has meant relearning the value of leisure. In their view, the empty porches of Newark Street reflect anything but successful living.

These are individuals who have, in several cases, reversed the clock on successful careers to achieve a kind of success that is so simple, even archaic, that in our modern madness we have forgotten it could easily be ours. They have opted to make time for the front porch and all its implications of a life that is full of imagination, meaning and connection to the larger community. They have learned to reinvent success on a slower and ultimately more satisfying track.

2

· ·

Images of Success

Remaking our image of success is one of the most important tasks of this book. To do that, however, we first need to understand the historical and modern-day forces that have shaped our notion of achievement and burned those images into our collective psyche.

There is little question that economic and societal changes during the past decade have intensified the pressures on professionals to work harder, aim higher and run faster than ever before. On the corporate front, global competition has all but eliminated the secure predictability of the executive suite as rapid technological innovations turn today's star performers into tomorrow's has-beens. Best-selling management books preach the importance of "loose" and "chaotic" organizations where new ideas come and go and goals change before the ink has dried on the next quarterly report.

Prospects of company mergers and downsizings of the management ranks have further intensified the insecurity among today's workers and fueled a nearly obsessive need to prove one's worth by taking on more projects and putting in longer hours. According to an American Management Association report, 39 percent of 1,084 organizations surveyed cut their work forces in the 12 months ending in June 1989; 35 percent did so during the same period the year before. Those remaining are expected to pick up the slack, take on more responsibility and put in longer hours. But even for those who do work the late nights and weekends, there is no guarantee of significant payoffs as efforts to cut costs and stay competitive by chipping away at the corporate bureaucracy result in fewer management layers of hierarchy and fewer rungs left to climb on the corporate ladder.

In a 1990 survey of some 200 CEOs, *Fortune* magazine found that although growing numbers of professionals were questioning the sanity of 60-hour work weeks, corporate leaders were calling for longer hours and an intensified devotion to the job. Seventy-seven percent said they felt American corporations would have to push their managers harder than ever in order to compete internationally. More than 50 percent of the CEOs said they expected high-level executives and middle managers to work an average of 50 to 59 hours a week, and 62 percent said executives in their companies were working longer hours than ten years before.[1] In such organizations, even the thought of pulling back can seem suicidal. Says AT&T supervisor Dick Muise: "This used to be a very stable place. But now that people are being let go on a regular basis, it's impossible not to feel insecure. There is a feeling that if you try to slow down a little, you may not be able to control how fast you do it—that someone else will control it for you. You could end up in some backwater operation somewhere or the organization might just decide that they don't need you at all."

One of the most dominant images of the eighties success culture was that of the once-proud company man forced to pound the pavement after years of dedicated service. The image suggested that it wasn't enough to be a loyal servant. Professionals who "made it" had to offer something extra-special. The result during the past decade has been an emphasis on professional success unheard of in previous generations. Back in the 1950s, 1960s and early 1970s, the biggest problem faced by corporations and other institutions was finding enough qualified people to fill managerial slots. The number of people in the labor force, most of whom were born during the Depression era, was at an all-time low, and relatively few were college-educated. During the baby boom years of 1946 to 1964, there was a sense of unlimited and automatic growth in this country. American productivity in the private sector advanced an average of 3.3 percent annually. From 1949 to 1959, a worker's real earnings grew by 63 percent. During the next ten years, that worker could still expect to see a 49 percent increase in earnings.

As a result, getting ahead and standing out hardly required working 60 to 70 hours a week. Those who performed well, usually within the context of a 40- or 50-hour week, were rewarded with a secure job and steady paycheck. If they were a touch more ambitious, if they wrote that extra report or came up with a particularly creative marketing plan, they would find themselves moving, with relative ease, up the organization. Today, the baby boom generation comprises the largest, best-educated work force in history. With fewer notches left to climb in the corporate hierarchy, simply emerging from the masses of other highly qualified workers requires a level of competitiveness that would have seemed outlandish to previous generations. Getting ahead economically, as well, is also far more of a struggle. A baby boomer entering the work force in the mid-1970s saw virtually no increase in real income ten years later. Given inflation, a 30-year-old male during the 1980s earned an average of 10 percent less than his father did, according to a report prepared for the Joint Economic Committee of Congress.

A history in fast forward

Current economic and demographic shifts have clearly made it more difficult for us to set limits. But our success imagery was formed long before the first baby boomers began to make their mark in the work force. Historically, this country has always equated progress with growth, and success with measurable forward movement. The further we traveled, the higher we climbed and the faster we did it, the greater our accomplishment. As a young nation, it was how we proved ourselves to a much more established European world.

In many ways, our pursuit up the next notch in the corporate hierarchy can be traced back to the days when this country took its first steps toward expansion and then set off on a tireless trek onward and upward. At no time was this more evident, notes James M. McPherson in his historical analysis of the Civil War, *Battle Cry of Freedom,* than during the first half of the nineteenth century, when the nation laid the practical and psychological foundations for a country on the move. In an approximately 50-year period, from about 1800 to 1850, the country's population and land size quadrupled. Our gross national product increased sevenfold. It was in these years that our notion of growth for growth's sake took hold. Overnight, America became the darling of the Western world, an upstart, precocious toddler whose sheer determination and energy had pushed it into young adulthood. "No other nation in that era could match even a single component of this explosive growth," writes McPherson. America became "the *Wunderkind* nation of the nineteenth century."[2]

The country grew quickly and impressively, barely taking the time to think about where it was headed or to plot its next step. "Regarded as 'progress' by most Americans, this unrestrained growth had negative as well as positive consequences," notes McPherson. The rights of Native Americans, blacks and women were pushed aside in the name of "progress," and the country plunged into its most deadly national crisis, the Civil War.[3]

In the decades that followed, America would continue to look for methods of speeding up its advancement in the eyes of the rest of the world. As the industrial age dawned, "efficiency" took center stage as the most vital ingredient of a progressive nation. The process of performing tasks smoothly and precisely quickly evolved into a science. "In less than 200 years, efficiency has risen from obscurity to become the overriding value of society and the primary method for organizing the activities of the human family," writes social theorist Jeremy Rifkin in *Time Wars.* [4]

Rifkin traces the growing emphasis on efficiency in modern Western society to three major economic innovations: division of labor, mass production, and the principles of scientific management. By assigning specific tasks to workers on the production floor, employers found more goods could be produced at a faster rate and at a cheaper cost. To make the division-of-labor process more efficient, the principles of mass production were introduced in the late eighteenth century. The heartbeat increased yet again with the introduction of scientific management. The focus was no longer on the efficiency of the process but the efficiency of the individual workers themselves. A stopwatch was used to measure worker performance within fractions of seconds to come up with time-saving changes. Every aspect of work, writes Rifkin, was defined by "the dictates of time. Worker performance could now be reduced to numbers and statistical averages that could be computed and analyzed to better predict future performance and to gain greater control over the work process itself."[5]

In most workplaces today efficiency is considered one of the most valued traits among successful professionals. The image of the superwoman and superman is essentially an image of superefficiency. The whole notion of time management is based on the idea that the quicker a task is completed, the better. Competence and efficiency, the thinking goes, are synonymous. But in glorifying efficiency for its own sake, not simply as a tool for helping us get the job done, we may lose track of what our true goals are and become detached from the intrinsic rewards of the work we are doing.

Not every culture places the same value on efficiency that we do. In a study conducted by researchers at California State University in Fresno, the only country that was shown to put a greater emphasis on time than the United States was Japan. Over the past decade we have come to view Japan as the country to emulate since, according to our own notion of progress, it is, indeed, surpassing us. The Japanese have brought to the workplace and everyday life new methods for mastering the art of speed and efficiency. If we are to continue to progress as a modern industrial power we must adopt their superior methods. Or so the thinking goes.

But what is superior? And what is progress? For Americans as individuals and as a society it has always been learning a task quickly and then moving on to the next one as rapidly as possible. But with each step forward our lives have become more complicated and our expectations about how long it should take us to make our mark as professionals less generous. The very speed with which we can accomplish a given task only makes the meaninglessness of the enterprise seem all the more glaring. If it takes so little time to get from here to there, are we really mastering anything but our own efficiency?

The toll of technology

Technology was supposed to unburden us. But it only seems to have increased the heartbeat, forcing us to absorb more information and put more time and energy into our work to keep up. All around us, the emphasis is on speed. We have computers that process information at a trillionth of a second. Our voice mail systems at work talk to our answering machines at home. The more information we can take in and the quicker we can process it, the better. When Carol Bartz, now vice-president of worldwide field operations for Sun Microsystems in Palo Alto, California, returned from a four-and-a-half-month maternity leave she was greeted with 12,000 pieces of electronic mail. "And those were just the informational messages. That number doesn't even include the notices for meetings or requests to solve a particular problem by next Thursday," says Bartz. "When you are handed all this information you feel you have to read it all and have an opinion on absolutely everything. You just get sucked in."

We have all been sucked in—even those of us who swore we would never be dependent on a computer. I remember my first newspaper job, writing away on an old manual Smith-Corona with keys that jammed if I typed more than 20 words per minute. When the first computers came to the newsroom, I resisted, never really taking the time to learn how to use them and pretending they were no more than fancy typewriters. Gradually, though, I was won over. Computers are quicker and easier.

But I also know that my own sense of how long it should take to complete a project has shrunk considerably during the past decade as I have become more closely connected with computer time. This struck me recently as I worked on this book.

I was staying at my sister's house in Denver for a few weeks to get away from the August heat and humidity of Washington, D.C. I had leased an IBM PC to write on while I was there and was perfectly happy with it—with one exception. It took about 60 seconds to boot up, twice as long as my Leading Edge back in Washington. I was impatient with the 30-second delay and even remarked to my brother-in-law that the computer seemed interminably slow. "How slow?" he asked. I told him about twice as slow as my computer at home. "How slow is that?" he wondered. When I explained the dramatic 30-second gap, he had a ready retort. "At that rate, you'll never get the book done."

Many psychologists believe that our growing connection with superefficient computer time is making us impatient and uncomfortable with the slower, more reflective nuances of life. If a task does not have a clear set of goals and explicit rewards, we feel we are not accomplishing anything. Craig Brod, an Oakland, California, psychologist who has studied computer-related stress, has found that many computer buffs, for instance, shun open-ended conversation. "They function much like a computer—they demand immediate feedback, limited downtime and have a short-term memory function," says Brod. "Their conversations end up being no more than information exchanges. Whereas true conversation is an open-ended process containing metaphor and subtlety, all they are after is straight detail."

Brod believes that these computer diehards are a frightening reflection of what is happening to society as a whole as we are continually deluged with new technological advances designed to make our lives easier and more efficient. Almost overnight, fax machines, car phones, checkout line scanners and instantaneous credit card access have become accepted and expected parts of everyday life. But in speeding up our daily routines, these innovations have also made us less patient and more comfortable with living on the surface. "After a meeting these days, I'll sometimes receive thank-you notes on the fax. The thinking seems to be, 'Why write a letter when you can create an instantaneous friendship this way?' " says Brod. In such a culture, whatever is most pressing—the report we have to finish, the meeting we have to get to—takes priority over activities that really matter far more to us than the task at hand. The speed with which tasks can be accomplished makes our work itself seem less satisfying and meaningful as we increasingly are forced to focus on the process of completing a project rather than the substance behind it.

The greatest irony, of course, is that we all assumed that computers would simplify our lives and give us more leisure time. Such notions now seem laughable. Consider the VDT operator who is now expected to perform 80,000 keystrokes per hour, compared with an average of 30,000 keystrokes back in the days of the typewriter. Or the architect who, using computer-aided design, can now, according to Brod, "make nineteen more decisions per hour than does a pencil-wielding colleague." Even normal conversation is being speeded up by the computer. Cassette tape recorders that use speech compression chips allow us to listen to a 60-minute cassette in half an hour. [6]

As the pace of the world around us quickens, we naturally adjust our lives and our attitudes to a new clock. The pressures we put on ourselves to complete a task, reach a goal, get a promotion have been intensified. The fax machine that allows us to move that sales document to the client in Tulsa in a matter of minutes would seem to give us more time for fine-tuning and revisions. In reality, it has only increased the client's expectations about how quickly he should receive the report. As one Seattle attorney put it: "Sure, computers and fax machines allow you to get the work done more quickly. The problem is, if you can do the job in half the time, the client is also going to pay you half as much. In order for the firm to stay financially viable, that means we have to take on more cases and bill more hours." The end result: The technical advances that have made our lives easier have only forced us to put in more time on the job and work harder to keep up.

Running the race in record time

There is little question that our societal tendency to confuse speed with success has been aggravated by a combination of economic, demographic and technological changes that seemed to reach a crescendo in the past decade. In its most extreme form, this pressure-cooker environment leads to an exaggerated image of success based on the kind of frenzied, self-destructive workaholism that has festered in Wall Street investment houses and high-powered law and consulting firms. It also typically results in burnout. The past decade saw a surge in the number of young professionals, often in their late 20s and early 30s, who suffered from depression, dissatisfaction and extreme physical fatigue. Many psychologists have noted the similarity of these symptoms to those generally associated with midlife crisis. For this group, it seems, everything was rushed—including their mental and physical breakdowns.

It was noon on a Wednesday when I first spoke with Matthew Simon. His voice sounded groggy when he answered the phone from his Belmont, Massachusetts, home, as if he had just woken up. Simon was 28 and had been bedridden for much of the last several months with a variety of flulike symptoms that his doctors diagnosed as chronic fatigue syndrome. "They say it's just a matter of taking care of myself and waiting. There isn't really much else I can do but rest," he explained. "Mostly I just feel tired and extremely weak, like I have the flu. Some days are better than others, but I basically feel this way every day to varying degrees."

From an early age, Simon measured his achievements by how much he could accomplish in the shortest period of time. "When he was interested in something, he was always interested in it up to his ears," recalled his mother, Mary Ann. Even as a boy, Simon, the youngest of four children, demonstrated a remarkable degree of intensity in whatever activity he was pursuing. "When he was five or six, I remember he was very interested in dinosaurs, like a lot of kids are at that age. But he had to immediately find out absolutely everything there was to know on the subject," said Mary Ann Simon. The young Simon's intensity accelerated when he got to college. While participating in several extracurricular activities, he received near-perfect grades at Williams College and was one of the few members of the junior class elected to Phi Beta Kappa. In his spare time, Simon ran a campus t-shirt business, founded and edited a campus political journal and was a junior adviser for a freshman dorm. When a student publication asked him how he managed to cram so much into his days and excel in so many areas, Simon had a ready reply, the irony of which is not lost today on the bedridden former fast-tracker: "I try not to sleep too much," he said then. "It's not only a waste of time, it's boring."

In a sense, people like Simon set a standard for all of us; they perpetuate the American notion that "anything is possible." If he could do it, so can we. If we give it our all, we too can perform astounding feats.

After graduating from college in 1982, Simon accepted what he describes as a "very high-powered, fast-paced job" with the Boston consulting firm Bain & Company. Simon, who had only a B.A. in political economy, was in the company of Harvard and Stanford business school graduates. There was plenty to keep him busy and challenged. But Simon's natural intensity and passionate desire for recognition led him to constantly search out new opportunities. Soon after arriving in Boston, he convinced his father to lend him the money to buy a brownstone in an up-and-coming neighborhood in the city's South End. The building had four apartments. Simon lived in one and rented out the other three. Suddenly he was in the real-estate business.

By 1984, Simon and a partner had bought ten buildings, renovated them and either rented them out or sold them as condos. "I was probably working a hundred hours a week at that point—full-time for Bain and full-time on the real-estate business," he recalls. Simon would typically spend the better part of his normal working hours at Bain on the phone, negotiating real-estate deals. He would then do the bulk of his number-crunching work for the consulting firm in the evening, usually not leaving the office before 11 p.m. But his day wasn't over yet. When he got home, Simon was usually up until two or three in the morning working on the real-estate business. The weekends and early morning hours before he went into the office were also reserved for looking at properties.

In the spring of 1984, Simon worked out a part-time schedule with Bain that would allow him to spend more time on the real-estate business. At that point, Simon had already struck it rich through real-estate deals. His net worth by age 24 exceeded $1 million. Financially, he didn't need Bain, but he was reluctant to give it up because it provided excellent contacts for his real-estate dealings. "I would be waiting in line at the copying machine and would end up selling a tax shelter to the guy standing next to me. I was able to raise a couple of million dollars that way."

The speed of Simon's success energized him. But he was like a gleaming new building constructed too hastily. The foundation was starting to crumble. Simon's part-time arrangement at the consulting firm called for him to be on the road in the Midwest three days a week visiting clients. Any time Simon passed a pay phone he would pull over and spend an hour or two negotiating a real-estate deal. He missed important meetings and started partying too heavily. After a night of bar-hopping with a young woman in Minnesota, Simon barely made an early morning flight back to Boston and then ended up sleeping through a transfer of planes in Detroit. He didn't wake up until the pilot announced that the plane was about to land in Philadelphia. "I was always pushing everything to the last minute because so much needed to be done," says Simon.

But the heavy load and high stress were starting to take a toll. Simon quit Bain completely and started working full-time on the real-estate business. Soon, though, he began looking for other challenges to fill his extra time. He attended a peer counseling workshop conducted by his mother, a psychotherapist, and discovered a new interest. Before long, Simon was spending 30 to 40 hours a week counseling, in addition to the 50 hours he put in managing real-estate properties. More often than not, though, Simon was merely going through the motions. "I was feeling emotionally burned out. The challenges that were once fun had just become an exhausting pain. I didn't work any less, it was just an exhausting pain in the ass. I worked myself into being very sick."

In March of 1988, after several months of fighting a flu he couldn't shake, Simon was diagnosed as having chronic fatigue syndrome. Frequently referred to as "yuppie mono," the illness is often associated with work-related stress and lasts at least six months and often for years. Although Simon continued working after the diagnosis, by August he was so sick that his doctors warned him he might do permanent damage to himself if he kept going. He sold out of the real-estate business and ceased being involved in the day-to-day management of properties. Simon has spent much of his time since then at home, resting and learning to relax. He writes poetry, reads books and has taught himself how to compose songs on his Casio keyboard. "I have written twenty songs in six months. I've read most of the classics and have written a stack of poems," he says. For Simon, even rest and relaxation have a quantifiable standard. "Somewhere along the line," he admits, "I got the message that you are judged on output and productivity and scores. I guess right now I have to figure out what it means to be me without relying on those external measures to define who I am."

Simon's case is not as extreme as it sounds. There are elements of Matthew Simon in almost all career climbers of the baby boom generation, although most of us do not have the stamina to maintain 80- to 100-hour work weeks for seven years. What we share with Simon is a desire to define ourselves through our jobs, to find personal fulfillment through work and to emerge from the masses of other bright, well-educated young achievers. For Simon, it wasn't the prospect of making more money that motivated him. It was, he says, "the feeling of being important, superior, standing out from the crowd." Stanley Rosenberg, of Dartmouth Medical School, believes that baby boomers like Simon are driven by a nearly all-consuming need for recognition. "Their fathers pursued a conformist ideal that went along with being a 1950s business executive—the Gregory Peck model. Everything from the make of car they drove to the hobbies they took up to the type of woman they married fit into this ideal. Baby boomers, by contrast, resist homogenization. They are looking to create completely new identities—to be extraordinary."

Yuppies and the culture of money

Being "extraordinary," of course, is easiest if one makes a lot of money and spends it extravagantly. Money in this country has always been our means of keeping score; of measuring our achievements in very clear, inarguable terms. As Alexis de Tocqueville wrote after visiting America more than a century and a half ago: "I know of no country, indeed, where the love of money has taken a stronger hold on the affections of men." As we neared the end of the twentieth century, that affection seemed to turn into lust.

In the 1980s, Americans went on an unprecedented spending spree. From 1983 to 1988, we bought 62 million microwave ovens, 57 million washers and dryers, 88 million cars and light trucks, 105 million color television sets, 46 million refrigerators and freezers, 63 million VCRs, 31 million cordless telephones and 30 million telephone answering machines. Debt accumulated, savings dwindled and still America kept buying.

The decade of the BMW, the condo, the Cuisinart and the yuppie is already beginning to seem like ancient history—the relics of a society that, at least for a time, seemed to go slightly berserk. But while the accumulation frenzy may have reached its peak, the emotional and economic climate that triggered it should not be so easily dismissed. In actual numbers, yuppies represented a small portion of the professional population—about 1.5 million people when factors such as lifestyle, occupation, age and income are taken into account.[7] This group's impact, however, cannot be measured in numbers alone. The yuppie, or the media depiction of the young urban professional, was the ultimate embodiment of our image of success. In an age

53

when simply buying a house was a struggle for the average middle-income professional, the much-maligned young MBA with his or her condo, BMW and penchant for extravagant vacations and expensive cheese created a new vision of the American Dream and a new set of goals to aspire to.

While our parents seemed to blend in with their neat lawns, practical cars and stable but unspectacular incomes, yuppies provided the clearest proof that this was a generation capable of creating its own identity and emerging from the middle-class masses. "I didn't want to be just another face in the crowd," said one former Chicago bond trader who was earning $200,000 a year by the time he was in his mid-20s. Although he grew up in an upper-middle-class environment and was always comfortable financially, the message he got from his parents was that success meant making more money than anyone else in his family. "I had an uncle who was very successful as an investment banker and I was always being compared with him. From an early age, I thought I would be a success if I made more money, got bigger deals and had a richer lifestyle than he did."

It is the American way. Our parents' generation had it better than their parents' generation. For us, success means having it better than those before us. But unlike our parents, who had their expectations shaped during the dismal years of the Depression and their achievements realized during the heady postwar period, this generation has had to contend with just the opposite. We were brought up to believe that there were certain material possessions that had to be accumulated and financial goals that needed to be met if we were to grow into successful, complete adults. That modest two-bedroom starter home with aluminum siding that suited our newlywed parents just fine would never do for us. We wanted to *start* in the house our parents traded up to—the three-bedroom with remodeled country kitchen, high ceilings and sprawling deck. That meant aiming higher and running faster than anyone before us.

Work as religion

Today's career climbers have never been willing to settle for what life handed them. Not only do we want a bigger house and a fancier car, we want careers that "mean something." Our parents, by comparison, seem to have wanted so little from their work. A career was something that provided security. It allowed them to pay for their kids' braces, piano lessons, summer camp and vacations at the shore. It was family that gave their lives meaning and provided them with a sense of identity.

For years I took for granted the professional sacrifices my own father made for my siblings and me. As a young cardiologist he had built a reputation in research. But the long hours and relatively low pay of an academic career, compared to private practice, were not conducive to building the type of family life he considered his number-one priority. Although research was my father's true love, he instead joined an internal medicine and cardiology practice with two other doctors that allowed him to set his own hours, spend evenings and weekends with his family and provide his children with the best educations and most comfortable upbringings. Work, however, was vitally important to my father—not so much because it gave him a sense of identity but because it provided him with the tools for building a rich family life based on the success imagery of the day.

The fact is, beneath the surface of the stereotyped uninvolved 1950s father, there has always been a rock-solid devotion to family values. The fifties imagery of emotional detachment and conformity has blinded many of us from appreciating our roots and understanding the importance of creating a successful family life. Instead, in many professions today, those brave enough to admit that family comes first, especially males, may end up placing themselves on a permanent career shelf. "My perception, when I was younger, was that people who talked about their families being more important than their careers were losers," says Matthew Lind (Chapter 6), who rose to group president of Mutual Life Insurance of New York, with an annual income of about $400,000, before deciding that family and personal well-being meant more to him than professional success.

What we do share with our parents is a fundamental devotion to work as a kind of personal and religious salvation. This modern American tendency to worship work has its roots in the Depression. It was during those years that Americans witnessed firsthand what life was like when jobs disappeared. Work was suddenly a precious commodity to be nurtured and treasured in much the way we now treat the few hours of leisure time we can salvage out of our hectic weeks. The Roosevelt administration reinforced this thinking by offering jobs, through the New Deal, as the answer to the country's economic woes. "Work provided a very specific and clear solution to the problems of the time. But it sent a message for years to come that more work for more people equaled progress," says Benjamin Hunnicutt of the University of Iowa.

Today, work has taken on the social function of a religion. Under this "theology of work," as Hunnicutt calls it, "such questions as 'Who am I? Where am I going? What am I doing here? What must I do to get out of the mess I'm in?'—historically religious questions—are answered by work." The result, notes Hunnicutt, is an unquestioning devotion to one's career.

This inflated notion of what a job should do for us has been reinforced, in recent years, by a number of social changes that seemed to find a convenient outlet in the workplace. The most obvious is the women's liberation movement, which turned the practical notion of a career into a symbolic battleground for equality and personal freedom. It was in the workplace that women would prove they were men's equals. The workplace would provide salvation for a generation of women who were bored, unchallenged and unappreciated. These high-flying notions about career fulfillment infiltrated the ideals and expectations of both male and female professionals who have entered the work force during the past two decades.

Further playing into these exaggerated expectations were the social changes brought about by the antiwar and civil rights demonstrations of the 1960s. This was, after all, a generation that had stopped a war and changed the course of history by refusing to play by the old rules. Even those who were not directly involved in these movements for change believed they were entitled to far more than what they perceived as the complacent, emotionally stultifying existences of their parents. They looked at the "organization men" of the 1950s and vowed to be different.

The workplace greeted their idealism and energy with open arms. In fact, dramatic philosophical changes were under way in corporate America that directly played into these exaggerated expectations. In the corporate setting, the 1960s counterculture movement was translated into a call for more humanistic management practices. In 1960, management theorist Douglas McGregor wrote a book called *The Human Side of Enterprise,* which challenged the prevailing belief that people had an innate dislike of work and would do the bare minimum necessary to get by unless they were controlled, coerced and manipulated to work harder. McGregor labeled this old approach Theory X and offered a new alternative—Theory Y. He argued that work was as natural as sleeping or playing and that if people were given clear and challenging objectives they would automatically push themselves to reach their highest potential. In an enlightened work environment, Theory Y held, work could be a primary source of ego gratification and personal development.[8]

Although many companies initially resisted the tenets of Theory Y, by the time today's professionals started entering the work force, its basic assumptions were already in place. Theory Y gave employers the perfect excuse for taking advantage of these eager young professionals. Work, after all, was no longer a burden to be finished up and forgotten as quickly as possible. It was a source of joy and inspiration. Career fulfillment, wrote Robert Townsend in *Up the Organization,* was a prerequisite to personal fulfillment. If companies recognized and encouraged employees' creative spirit and drive to succeed, the result would be a work force willing, even eager, to put their professional lives before their personal ones. Under such thinking, it was perfectly acceptable for work to "come between a man and his family," noted Townsend. Of the then typically male employee, he wrote, "You want him to enjoy his work so much he comes in on Saturday instead of playing golf or cutting the grass."[9] In many professions today, it is almost a given that people will work evenings and weekends. Said one public relations manager in Minneapolis: "My boss is always calling meetings on Saturdays. I don't like it, but I don't really question it either. Making an appearance shows that I am devoted to my job."

On the surface at least, the workplace of the past 30 years has offered new outlets for creative expression. The human potential movement of the sixties and seventies found a home in the workplace in the form of T-groups, encounter sessions and corporate team development programs. Through "participative management" techniques, efforts were made to free organizations from bureaucratic constraints and create an atmosphere where everyone could share in decisionmaking. Despite all the talk and publicity that these new approaches generated, little of substance had actually changed. By 1980, only 15 percent of companies with 100 or more employees had human resource programs, according to the New York Stock Exchange's Office of Economic Research. Instead, many companies used "new age" management techniques as a quick fix to boost morale and productivity.

Still, expectations had already been built up by all the hype and inflated promises. MBA courses and best-selling management books glorified what, in reality, were only a handful of companies that had made substantive changes. But those entering the work force naturally assumed they were lucky enough to be starting careers during a new age of enlightenment. What they discovered instead were work environments that had become harder-edged, more numbers-oriented and more competitive than ever before. While one arm of the corporate bureaucracy had been assembling human resource departments and putting together executive encounter groups, the other arm had essentially been knocking them down with a variety of new technical theories that attempted to quantify organizational planning and management into a science. Under the new "technocratic" mentality, everything was reduced to a number and a flow chart. "Personnel representatives, rather than listening to people, began to study the results of corporate attitude surveys," which attempted to quantify the needs of an entire work force on a few sheets of paper, note Donald L. Kanter and Philip H. Mirvis in *The Cynical Americans*.[10]

The mixed messages coming from the corporate world had a significant impact on those entering the work force in the 1970s and set the stage for the self-absorption and workaholism of the 1980s. On one hand, the humanistic movement called for more independence and less adherence to traditional rules, while the technocratic approach promoted greater emphasis on cold logic and a rock-hard bottom line. Emerging from this hypocrisy was the hero of the modern-day corporate arena—

Michael Maccoby's "gamesman."[11] The gamesman combined extreme independence with a calculating "every man for himself" attitude. He played by the rules, as Kanter and Mirvis point out, as long as he could create his own.[12]

In the past decade, the dynamic work environments of so-called baby boomer companies, most notably the high-stakes, high-tech firms of Silicon Valley and Route 128 outside of Boston, provided a perfect breeding ground for such attitudes. These communities of work preached both self-actualization and quantifiable results, and their message was intoxicating to the masses of driven, highly educated young professionals looking to make their mark. On the surface, "intrapreneurial" environments held out an irresistible promise of creativity and control. But what many professionals have discovered is that the very looseness of such organizations reinforced a system in which professionals were forced to continually top their own achievements, to outshine themselves before a competing team or company did. As a result, rather than bringing more control, each new success generated more work and more of a sense that the pace of the job had taken on a life of its own.

"When the company is growing so fast and you are constantly being told how important your work is, it feels impossible to just back off," says Deborah Coleman, the former chief financial officer of Apple Computer. By her early 30s, Coleman was already the highest-ranking female executive in Silicon Valley. But physical and mental fatigue, including a serious weight problem, led her to take a leave of absence in the winter of 1989 and ultimately return to the company in a lesser role. In a conversation shortly before her return, Coleman told me she had wanted to pull back for some time but felt paralyzed by her own success and that of the rapidly expanding company. "We had just finished this six-month full court press. I was traveling constantly and was in these meetings day after day that would last from seven a.m.

to seven p.m. There was no way to ever take a breath. Then phase two of the project started up right after that. I had to stay focused and energetic. I couldn't even take a break. I felt like I wasn't in control of myself at all anymore."

In such an atmosphere, it is easy to lose touch with the outside world and come to view one's professional environment as a complete family—a community of work. Best-selling management theory has reinforced such notions by advertising the workplace as a maker of dreams and purveyor of personal visions. The entrepreneurial evangelism and "excellence" movements of the 1980s played into the notion of career as religion. The bible was the corporate mission statement, which gave every worker a common purpose and clear set of values. The corporate theologian was the podium-pounding, red-faced entrepreneurial visionary/salesman who preached the gospel of both self-fulfillment and getting rich quick. This role was perfected by such success stories as Victor Kiam of Remington and Minnesota entrepreneur Harvey Mackay, author of *Swim with the Sharks*.

In the past decade, all of this has held a particular appeal for disenchanted young professionals looking for a sense of meaning and community. Talk of building strong corporate cultures where employees and management worked together toward common goals and ideals seemed the perfect antidote for professionals whose lives lacked continuity and stability. In an age when family and societal values were increasingly flimsy, the workplace held out hope for a kind of personal and spiritual salvation. The divorce rate had doubled during the postwar period and professionals, in pursuit of the best educations and best job opportunities, were separated both geographically and emotionally from larger community and family values. "My profession was the one thing I felt I had control over," recalls Eleanor Wachs, who became increasingly detached from her traditional upbringing as she focused more of her energies on building a successful career.

In reality, of course, mergers, acquisitions and downsizings have turned the workplace into anything but a secure and stable community. Kanter and Mirvis contend that today's corporate revivalism contains a strong element of "smoke and mirrors" that allows companies to manipulate employees with empty promises and false illusions of grandeur. "That some organizations have developed more humane and inspiring work cultures has further fired the imagination," write Kanter and Mirvis. "What so many people have encountered, instead, is that the grim realities of economic life . . . limit their possibilities and make corporate promises of self-fulfillment illusory."[13]

Ideally, it is the opportunity to exercise one's creativity and perform intellectually challenging tasks that compels professionals to eat and breathe work. And, certainly, there are times when the rewards of a job well done are more than worth the tradeoffs. In reality, however, what has turned so many career climbers into workaholics during the last two decades is a system that rewards those who play the best politics, endure the most grueling schedules and contribute most directly to the bottom line. The result is not happiness and satisfaction but obsession, exhaustion and burnout.

Looking to our employers for answers

One thing is clear: We cannot expect corporate America to solve our problems. As we have seen, with more competition and more pressures on the bottom line, management expects us to increase our hours on the job, not decrease them. Many of us, however, seem intent on waiting for a new company policy or program to show us the way to happier and more satisfying lives. We may be waiting a long time.

Much has been written in the popular press over the past few years about the new enlightened management policies. More organizations are providing day care, flexible work schedules and a host of other services to help professionals with families and interests beyond work lead more balanced lives. In reality, however, while a handful of companies have made genuine attempts to confront shifting societal values and address individual needs, the overall assumptions about success and progress in a career remain unchanged.

Instead, the vast majority of companies have merely adopted a policy or two, while making little or no attempt to change deep-seated corporate attitudes. Arlene Johnson, a senior researcher for The Conference Board, a business and economics research organization in New York, estimates that under 50 companies nationwide have comprehensive programs for addressing work-family issues. "These are companies that not only have programs for childcare and eldercare, but are also working to change the corporate culture with sensitivity training for managers and other similar efforts," says Johnson.

But even having such programs is no guarantee of real change, particularly if individuals in the workplace continue to cling to a narrowly focused image of success. Such arrangements as part-time and flextime, for example, while helpful in the short term, often end up being little more than superficial remedies if those taking advantage of them fail to place realistic limits on their jobs. In fact, "flexibility" has become a kind of quick-fix cure for overburdened professionals who mistakenly believe that shifting the hours of the work day will magically make their lives more manageable and satisfying.

In its most extreme form, the promise of flexibility leads to the dangerous assumption that one can truly "do it all." Steven

Klimczak figured that if he could just leave the office early enough to spend evenings with his two young daughters, he would find a way to get all his work done. So Klimczak, who as director of treasury for Merck & Company's international operations frequently puts in a 65- to 70-hour week, set a new "flexible" schedule for himself: He started leaving the office every day promptly at 5 p.m., about two or three hours before most people in his department, picking up his eldest daughter at the nearby day care center and devoting the early evening hours to his family, including helping his wife Janet get the girls ready for bed and reading to them as they fell asleep. "It has always been important to me to be an active parent," says Klimczak. "I never saw the point of having children if you didn't play a big role in raising them yourself."

In order to manage both his active parenting role and demanding professional career, however, Klimczak paid a heavy price. He worked nearly every evening after his daughters went to sleep and set his alarm for 3:30 or 4 a.m. each night so he could put in three more hours of work at home and make up for his "early" exit from the office. Although the schedule allowed Klimczak to continue to shine on the job and devote time to his family as well, it ultimately left him feeling empty, exhausted and dissatisfied. "I was tired all the time and felt like I had absolutely no time for myself," recalls Klimczak. In the end, his attempt at flexibility turned Klimczak's life into little more than a physically and emotionally draining triumph over scheduling that left him with almost no time for joy or reflection, let alone sleep.

Even part-time work, a wonderful alternative for many professionals, can create more problems than it solves unless the position is realistically recast within the confines of a limited schedule. Valerie Fisher's experience was typical. "I was getting 50 percent of my salary and supposedly working three days a week, but I couldn't expect the business world to come to a halt during my days off," says the Chicago attorney, who went on a part-time schedule at her former law firm following the birth of her third child, before leaving to open her own firm with two other women (Chapter 6). "I found it very difficult to ever really feel relaxed about it. If I was at the grocery store or taking the kids to the zoo during one of my alleged days off, I would have to call the office every hour. There was absolutely no mental freedom."

It is worth noting that Fisher's previous employer, Sachnoff & Weaver, is generally considered one of the most flexible law firms in Chicago. And Klimczak's employer, Merck & Company, is frequently cited by human resource professionals as among the most progressive corporations in the country when it comes to dealing with such issues as working parents and childcare. Still, unless professionals make the mental shift and structure their jobs to coincide with their new schedules, such setups as part-time and flextime will not allow them to take control of their lives. The problem is that no matter how enlightened, most large organizations continue to define success in the narrowest of terms and reward forms of behavior that run counter to building happy lives and healthy personal relationships. More often than not, that means glorifying destructive workaholic behavior.

In fact, achieving success in most companies today requires sublimating those traits that we may value most. What Michael Maccoby in *The Gamesman* refers to as qualities of the heart—compassion, generosity, courage, the capacity to love—are discouraged and underdeveloped on the typical corporate career track in favor of purely intellectual and analytical characteristics.[14] But we have come to equate the ability to adapt within such organizations as vital to leading normal and successful lives. We judge our own achievements according to how skillfully we follow the path laid down by those ahead of us, those who have made it within this system.

A growing chorus of psychologists finds this trend disturbing. They have concluded that rather than representing an ideal to which we should strive, those individuals who are adapting and seemingly thriving on the fast track are often the least emotionally stable individuals of all, although on the surface they may seem to be gliding smoothly through life. In *Modern Madness: The Emotional Fallout of Success,* Douglas LaBier, a Washington, D.C., therapist, concludes that "career winners"—professionals who have risen quickly and seemingly painlessly in their fields—are frequently motivated by a selfish and unhealthy lust for power and personal recognition. He gives examples of highly successful professionals, such as one executive who enjoyed "cracking the whip" every now and then "just for the fun of it," and a top-level government bureaucrat who liked to brag about his exploits at undermining a superior and eventually contributing to his departure. [15] While such individuals represent an extreme, the fact remains that they have been rewarded for behavior that most of us would consider at the very least distasteful. Because of their clear and measurable professional success, we glorify them as models of fast-track achievement.

By contrast, the more psychologically healthy individuals, those who form the heart of this book, may appear for a time to have a great deal of trouble adjusting to the career culture that has allowed them to become so successful. They are, says LaBier, "basically normal inside" but have taken such pains to mold themselves onto an unnaturally narrow career track that they feel depressed and dissatisfied. Still, they continue to push ahead, typically believing that their inability to adapt is the source of their dissatisfaction. For lack of other apparent options, they cling to the belief that making more money and gaining more power are synonymous with happiness. The result is a profound sense of disappointment. Although their lives seem the embodiment of success in our culture, they feel bewildered and genuinely sad.

Creating our own success imagery

Moving ahead on a career track will always be an important part of the success equation for many of us. Work is our anchor—it tells us who we are and whether we measure up financially, creatively and intellectually. But in our quest to conform to a predetermined image of success, we have lost track of our true goals: to lead meaningful and worthwhile lives. We have allowed our careers to control us.

Pulling back will, of course, require making sacrifices, the most obvious of which are financial. In terms of pure monetary and lifestyle impact, however, those sacrifices may be surprisingly minimal. Rather than moving backwards economically, the majority of downshifters merely end up plateauing their lifestyles. They learn to live without a remodeled kitchen, a new car every five years and that bigger dream house they once believed they had to have. Instead, they come to appreciate the comforts and sense of belonging that results from staying put. Money, they begin to see, matters far less when they are personally and professionally satisfied.

The downshifters you will meet in the next five chapters were chosen from among more than 100 professionals interviewed in preparation for this book, representing a variety of fields, work environments and regions of the country. But they inevitably share a common philosophy: They have come to feel that setting limits for themselves does not make them less successful or less worthy than their colleagues who continue to sacrifice their evenings, weekends and personal happiness to complete another report or project. Reinventing success for them means rethinking the imagery that has influenced so many of their professional goals and ambitions; it means being guided by their own individual notions of life success.

3

· ·

The Plateauer

Linda Greenhouse was 14 years old when her image of professional success took hold. It was 1961, the year John F. Kennedy entered the White House, and Greenhouse read Theodore H. White's riveting account of life on the campaign trail, *The Making of the President—1960.* For the next 25 years, recalls Greenhouse, "I carried around this romantic ideal of myself as a newspaper reporter racing from planes to buses to hotel rooms with a trenchcoat slung over my shoulder and a notebook in my hand."

That image influenced her decision to go into journalism after graduating from Radcliffe College. It fueled Greenhouse's career as a young reporter for the *New York Times,* where she covered the state house in Albany while still in her 20s and then the U.S. Supreme Court as a correspondent in the newspaper's Washington, D.C., bureau. In 1986, Greenhouse finally had the opportunity to fulfill her dream and take to the road for a year covering the presidential campaign. But to her surprise, she found herself resisting. "White's book had shaped my perception of what journalism was all about and what I wanted to be for so long that I just assumed I would follow that path," she recalls.

Both practically and emotionally, however, Greenhouse had been pulling away from the image of herself as a reporter on the campaign trail. On the practical side, she now had a young daughter and a husband who she couldn't imagine leaving behind for the better part of a year as she played out her adolescent fantasy. Perhaps even more importantly, Greenhouse had come to realize that the old vision of herself had little to do with her true passions. In fact, her professional aspirations and dreams were being met every day as she pored through important legal decisions in her cramped pressroom cubicle at the Supreme Court and translated them into clear, insightful prose for the newspaper. "The kind of in-depth analysis I am able to do covering the court is in many ways more rewarding to me and more suited to my own intellectual pace than the glamorous life of the trenchcoat and overnight bag," says Greenhouse.

It was those combined considerations that ultimately gave Greenhouse the strength to say "no." She continued to hang on to her dream in the months after she made her decision, telling herself that other opportunities would come up in future elections; that she would then be willing to make the personal sacrifice. In reality, however, Greenhouse knew she had shut the door on a piece of herself. Rather than being controlled by a 14-year-old's vision of success, Greenhouse realized that sometimes our success imagery needs revising; that the pictures in our current lives often contain the clearest and most satisfying images of all.

Winning versus succeeding

Most notions of success in our culture fall into two distinct categories. The first type, which is frequently glorified in movies, tv shows and best-selling books, equates achievement with the singular goal of "winning." In his book *Confessions of an S.O.B.*, Gannett Company chairman Allen H. Neuharth puts it succinctly: "Winning is the most important thing in life. And the most rewarding. Everything pales in comparison to the feeling of winning."[1] On the career front, this version of success inevitably involves chasing an endless series of external goals such as promotions and raises.

By contrast, the second type of success is usually slower, more carefully considered and less glamorous. It is characterized by people like Greenhouse, who throughout her career has turned down promotions and adjusted her notion of achievement to coincide with a broader definition of success that encompasses personal, spiritual and intellectual needs.

It is this view that provides the success framework for the plateauer. But it is a philosophy that does not fit neatly into a culture that routinely glorifies the type of success personified, to an extreme, by people like Neuharth. Creating an image of professional success that does not automatically include promotions, for instance, means separating oneself from some of the most basic notions of career achievement in our culture. On a personal level, when there are no external rewards to point to, friends, family and colleagues may wonder what plateauers are up to and why they don't appear to be progressing in their careers. Living without promotions may also mean hitting a financial plateau: The big bonuses and raises typically aren't handed out to those who set a reasonable professional pace and don't regularly jockey for position on the corporate success ladder.

Within an organization a promotion is inarguably the most valued reward. "Unlike verbal praise or a symbolic pat on the head, it's a put up or shut-up response: either you get it or you don't. . . . It's the essence of recognition and affirmation because it results in more power," writes Judith M. Bardwick in *The Plateauing Trap.* [2]

Even when we try to convince ourselves that promotions don't really matter, it's hard not to feel a twinge of jealousy when a colleague gets one and we don't. Nothing, after all, feeds the ego quite like a promotion—not a fancier office, a more interesting assignment or even a heftier paycheck. "A promotion is the ultimate form of recognition," says Mark Deschere, a chemical engineer for Du Pont who has been turning down offers to move to the corporate suite for several years. But Deschere is the first to admit that learning to live without the regular reinforcement of a new and more impressive job title isn't easy. "Being handed more power just feels good. It's much harder to feel successful when the rewards are primarily internal." Bardwick takes that thinking a step further: "Promotion is a judgment that usually involves the core of how we feel about ourselves. When it is offered, our image of our core self is confirmed." [3]

More often than not, however, promotion is not about ambition. It is about competition and, as such, tends to reinforce our most adolescent instincts. We want to be a member of the club, to fit in and be accepted by our peers. Getting a promotion means we are one of the chosen few—the most popular boys and girls in the class, the star athletes, the most likely to succeed. Although a promotion can be a deeply valued reward resulting from specific professional achievements, in many cases a promotion's meaning is far less worthy: It is about winning, pure and simple. But if the only thing that matters is that we win, we have nothing else to give our lives substance. Consequently, rewards such as promotions become all-important. "When winning is *everything*," notes Bardwick, "people get themselves into psychological trouble. If they're not winners, what are they?"[4] In Neuharth's case, for example, the pursuit of "winning" drove him to act as a newsroom spy in order to land a job with the *Miami Herald*, conspire to unseat his former boss at Gannett and brazenly stamp out those who threatened his efforts to build the world's largest newspaper empire.[5]

There will always be room, perhaps even a need, for the Neuharth version of success. For most of us, however, tailoring our ambitions and professional careers to such a restrictive notion of achievement will prove dissatisfying. The answer, for a growing number of professionals, is plateauing. More of them are saying "no" to promotions that would take them away from the work they love most and turn up the stress level several notches. They are turning down opportunities for advancement that would lengthen the work day and detract from their personal and family time. And in vastly increasing numbers they are refusing to relocate even if it means disrupting their career advancement.

Traversing the lateral ladder

Not so long ago, "plateauer" was a kinder, gentler word for deadwood. In the corporate world, the plateaued were typically middle managers whose solid but unspectacular performance allowed them to coast comfortably toward retirement while making a minimal contribution to the organization. Today, plateauers are no longer synonymous with deadwood, and the opportunity to stay in place and avoid the political entanglements of the upward track may actually lead to new opportunities for creative and intellectual development.

What the old notion of plateauing does share with the updated version is an assumption that traditional advancement up the corporate ladder is no longer a given. Today, more professionals than ever, and at an increasingly early age, are finding themselves among the ranks of the newly plateaued. Their numbers continue to grow as companies chip away at layer after layer on the corporate hierarchy, resulting in fewer steps left to climb and a considerably reduced number of promotions to compete for. At General Electric, for example, 20 out of 29 management layers have been eliminated by the company.[6] Winning and succeeding in such organizations, by necessity, means something very different than it did in the old vertical bureaucracies. Rather than measuring one's progress by moving ahead in one narrow area, success in such companies may now involve traversing a lateral path from, say, a sales role to a communications job to a human resources position, gaining new expertise and higher compensation with each shift. While the flattening hierarchy means midlevel employees will have more responsibility than those before them, it also means that with fewer layers above them to contend with, they will have more control over the day-to-day management of their careers.

By contrast, confining one's career to a narrow upward career track can actually limit choices and make it more difficult to do the type of work one enjoys most. In fact, in many companies today, plateauing actually opens up opportunities for those who wish to focus on the technical or creative aspects of their fields, rather than the managerial. For Mark Deschere, plateauing has led to professional and personal challenges that would have proven elusive if he had stuck to the traditional corporate management track.

In the summer of 1978, Deschere found himself "pacing

the floor" during a brief corporate assignment at Du Pont head-
quarters in Wilmington, Delaware. This was where he was supposed to be; this was his reward for being a talented,
hard-working engineer. The problem was, Deschere was no longer allowed to be an engineer and perform the type of work that
had been his passion ever since he could remember. As a child,
Deschere loved nothing more than pulling apart radios, telephones, anything he could get his hands on—and then figuring
out how to put them back together again.

When Deschere realized he could turn his hobby into a
career, it was icing on the cake. "For me, the greatest thrill of all
is seeing the tangible results of my work. I get a tremendous
sense of joy and satisfaction when I walk down a grocery store
aisle and see sitting right there on the shelf products I played a
part in producing," says Deschere. But in the world Deschere was
quickly headed toward—the corporate suite—he would be dealing in paper, not products. "Once you are in an executive position you no longer go out and smell and feel and touch the
product. You simply direct others to do it," says Deschere, who
is in his early 40s.

It was during his stint in Wilmington that Deschere decided the traditional fast track was never going to take him where
he wanted to go. Like many technically and creatively skilled
people, however, he was torn between the desire to move up in
the organization and his own sense of what would make him most
comfortable with his life and his work. When he looked inward,
Deschere saw a success imagery that had never wavered and had
always been based on his pure love of engineering. "My mother
always said that although all three of her sons became engineers,
I was the only *real* engineer."

Throughout his career, Deschere's professional role models also reflected a notion of success that seemed to be pointing
him in a direction other than the executive management ranks.

As a young employee at Du Pont, Deschere found that the person he respected and idolized most was not toiling away in the corporate suite but was a well-rounded professional engineer who stayed close to the nitty-gritty of the job and the people most directly involved in the manufacturing process. Having such a role model in mind helped Deschere keep his true goals in constant view.

The most important professional role models, however, are not always the most obvious ones. Carolyn McCormick, who jumped the partnership track at Andersen Consulting in Chicago to pursue a career on the less upwardly mobile administrative side of the business in the firm's Washington, D.C., office, found that one of her most significant models for making the move was her father—a classic 1950s-style organization man. "He was part of an era and culture where you just stayed put at the same company for life. But when I was ten and he was about to be made a partner at Price Waterhouse, he decided to leave the company and take a less consuming corporate job, in large part because he wanted to have more time to devote to his family. I realize now what an important message that sent to me." As we will see throughout this book, much of the fifties imagery that so many of us routinely disdain contains important lessons that may help us refocus our lives today.

Typically, the people we choose as role models are those who have achieved traditional success and have been showered with the traditional rewards of upward mobility. Young professionals are taught to model their lives after these fast-trackers from an early stage, to search for a mentor who will teach them the political game and guide them in their careers.

The temptations of that path to the top—the promise of prestige, recognition and wealth—were never far from Deschere's world as a young engineer at Du Pont. What enabled him to pull away from those temptations were a combination of spiritual beliefs, which stressed the importance of using one's "god-given talents to make a difference," and a growing awareness that the world he was headed toward was occupied by a lot of frustrated people who felt trapped by their professional success. "I believe we are all here for a reason, to make a contribution. But I was falling into the trap of constantly setting objectives for myself and then moving on to the next one. All that left me with was a feeling of going from objective to objective. I didn't want to end up in some corporate job, pushing papers and never knowing if I was really contributing to anything."

Today, Deschere no longer relies on institutional objectives to measure and guide his professional achievements. Instead, for the last several years, he has thrived as a plateauer at Du Pont, building an exciting and stimulating career for himself through a series of lateral moves. Since his career success is not guided by the race for the next promotion, Deschere has more time to focus on the substance of his work and the sheer sense of accomplishment that comes from seeing a project through from beginning to end, rather than measuring his achievements by how quickly and efficiently he advanced to the next task. "One of the frustrations of promotion is that you don't get to see the results of the work you're doing because you are promoted out of it," says Deschere. "The higher you get, the longer it takes for you to see and feel the impact of your work."

Staying put in the same job for five years as a manufacturing superintendent at the company's polymers plant in Parkersburg, West Virginia, allowed Deschere to take part in each phase in the development of a new plastics engineering facility. "I was there to start the program, go through the development stage, authorize the program, put people to work on it, turn it over and then start reporting on the results. And the results have been very good. I glow with pride now when I read the weekly reports about what our group did. If I accepted a promotion, I would have gotten away from it long before we even saw the results or were able to do any followup."

In his search for new challenges, Deschere recently made another lateral move to senior engineering associate with the company's Freon alternatives program. Deschere coordinates the development of a manufacturing plant that will produce an "ozone-friendly Freon" for such products as air conditioners and refrigerators. Once again, Deschere is maintaining a direct involvement in the engineering process, with the added bonus of working on something he believes in. As he enthusiastically puts it: "It feels fantastic to be doing something that has enormous potential for the good of mankind."

In exchange for greater professional challenges and more control over his career, Deschere, of course, has had to learn to live without any promotions at all. Although his salary is also not what it would have been in a corporate position, regular raises and occasional bonuses help fulfill Deschere's need for outward recognition. "The only regular sign I get now that the company is happy with me is a pay increase," says Deschere. "It has nothing to do with the actual money. It is just the fact that I am being rewarded in some way."

Those monetary rewards also help Deschere contend with the occasional comments from colleagues who can't understand why he hasn't been promoted and the emotional upheaval that inevitably accompanies the promotion of a close friend or colleague. "I had tracked career paths with one guy for a long time and we were very close. To see him move up and not me was difficult."

Deschere believes he may always have to fight such internal battles. But that is a price he is more than willing to pay. In Deschere's case, rather than closing off his options, plateauing has given him more choices and more control over his professional life. "If I had gone the corporate route and continued to accept promotions, I wouldn't have been able to move as freely and explore new technologies," he says. Basing his career on lateral moves rather than promotions has also allowed him to circumvent what he sees as a growing frustration among many of his colleagues who took the traditional corporate path. "There is only so high that they are going to go at this point. Some are already starting to feel the effects of the flattened organization. They are bored and frustrated because they gave up the exciting hands-on work for the temporary rewards of moving up. But those rewards are no longer there for them." By following his own success imagery, rather than that provided by the corporation, Deschere has been able to build a career for himself that is inherently meaningful and satisfying.

Putting limits on high-stress careers

Creating and following a personal success path means learning to set work patterns that reinforce rather than sabotage our deepest notions about what constitutes a successful life. This is more difficult than it sounds. Even if we know what we want from our careers, the pressures to always strive for more are difficult to resist. More power, more money, more prestige are the essence of success in our culture. These exaggerated goals push us to accept jobs we don't particularly want and take on more responsibility than we can reasonably handle.

There is little question that many professionals feel they work hard enough already and, given the option, would prefer to refine their current skills rather than take on more and more responsibility. In 1989, the executive search firm Korn/Ferry International surveyed 700 senior executives at Fortune 500 companies and found that only 47 percent wanted to add to their responsibilities compared with 58 percent ten years ago. But the higher one climbs, the more hours one is expected to devote to the job. According to the 1990 *Fortune* magazine poll, the average CEO works 61 hours a week. Many, of course, put in far more hours than that.

In today's competitive business environments, 70- and 80-hour work weeks are often more than a test of macho endurance. Global competition and rapid technological advancements have crippled some of the most venerable American corporations. Staying a step ahead of the competition in the computer or telecommunications businesses, for instance, requires considerably more than nine-to-five days for career-climbing technicians and managers.

Skyrocketing overhead costs and fierce competition for a leaner client base have forced even once genteel professions like law to assume the ruthlessness of corporations. It used to be that an attorney who made partner at a law firm was secure for life—as an owner of the practice, he or she couldn't be fired. No more. Today, keeping firms afloat requires that partners wear several hats, including salesperson, marketing expert and business manager, not to mention skillful attorney. Making partner and staying partner means mastering all those diverse skills and working longer hours than ever. A partner in a major Chicago law firm, for instance, currently is expected to bill about 2,100 hours a year. That figure was closer to 1,600 hours in the mid-1980s. Furthermore, the partnership title no longer gives one the luxury of easing back a bit. These days, the once unheard-of practice of firing partners has become common procedure.

It is in such high-pressure fields that the fear of slowing down is greatest—and the need most intense. The culture of overwork and busyness that typifies these professions is viewed as an unalterable fact of life. I have a friend, a consultant in the high-tech industry, who insists that at his company it is easier to work seven days a week than to "suffer the consequences" of turning down an occasional assignment or asking for a weekend off. "You don't understand," he explains, having just canceled another dinner date. "There really isn't anything I can do. It's like this for *everyone.* If I could do something about it I would. I don't like working this much. I hate it."

But even where there is seemingly "no way out"—even in professional environments where the demands are so great as to seem inescapable—there is always another way, as long as we are willing to set limits for ourselves. The fear my friend feels, and the fear we have all felt to varying degrees at one time or another, stems from a belief that if we alter the rules of the game even slightly we will be branded as misfits, troublemakers or lazy. Instead, we automatically take the course laid out by those before us, since, at the very least, we know it won't get us fired. But if we use a little creativity and imagination, and learn that we are unlikely to shatter a leg if we occasionally put a foot down, a surprising number of choices will open up to us.

At law firms, for instance, the typical attorney still sees the only road to success as the partnership track—the old "up or out" mentality. In reality, most large firms and a growing number of smaller firms have had options in between for several years now. At many firms, for instance, those willing to trade in the financial rewards of owning a piece of the firm for the less stressful but by no means low-paying role of "nonequity" or "income" partner will almost certainly be able to achieve a saner balance. Setting limits, of course, always means making tradeoffs. At large firms, partners with a financial stake in the business earn anywhere from about $200,000 annually to as much as $1 million in places like New York and Chicago. The average income for a salaried partner with no shares in the business would probably be in the $150,000 to $200,000 range. In exchange for the lower but hardly poverty-level income, such an attorney would typically not have to bill as many hours as a full partner and would be able to focus more on practicing the law, rather than socializing with potential clients and bringing in new business.

As a full partner for the Boston law firm Gaston & Snow, Stuart Rossman says he would be expected to bill at least 2,300 hours annually. As an income partner, however, he has maintained a far more manageable 1,800 to 1,900 hours, leaving him time to chair the firm's pro bono committee and maintain a heavy involvement in outside community affairs and an active family life. Accepting a nonequity position has in no way closed off Rossman's options should he feel more tempted in the future by the economic rewards of partnership. In the three years he has been an income partner, Rossman, who is in his mid-30s, has seen several members of his class move on to full partnership from the nonequity slot. He has not ruled out the possibility himself of making a push for shareholder status sometime in the future. For now, however, Rossman, a real-estate litigation specialist, believes he has the best of all worlds. "In every sense of the word, except for compensation, I am a partner. What the lower income gives me is the flexibility to have a life beyond work."

Professionals like Rossman are not shy about voicing their priorities. "It is up to me to set limits and say how far I am willing to go. I have let the firm know exactly where I stand," says Rossman. Plateauers who set limits in competitive fields possess an unusual degree of self-confidence. They typically have a strong sense of their professional worth combined with an innate understanding that they are more than the sum of their professional parts.

Having paid their dues for the first decade or so of their careers, plateauers believe they should be rewarded not with ever-expanding hours on the job but with the ability to make the kind of choices people like Rossman and Linda Greenhouse have made. Before joining the Washington bureau of the *New York Times,* Greenhouse spent four years commuting from New York City to Albany, where she covered the state house for the newspaper, usually leaving her apartment early Monday morning and returning late Friday. "Major legislation routinely wasn't brought to the floor until after midnight. I worked a lot of long hours and did an estimable job. When I came to Washington, I felt I had paid my dues and could now take charge of my career," says Greenhouse.

But even several years after proving their value to a company, many career professionals continue to put up with increasingly demanding workloads and growing unhappiness with the type of work they have been promoted into. Linda Greenhouse's career perspective stems, in large part, from her place in a "transitional generation," a generation in which a career was still something of a rarity for women, not the linchpin of one's identity. It is that perspective, perhaps more than anything else, that has given Greenhouse the ability to maintain a remarkably balanced life in one of the most high-pressure, competitive work environments imaginable.

When Greenhouse went to work for the *Times* in the late sixties, she wasn't so much driven by ambition as curiosity. "I was twenty-two and just thought it was neat," says Greenhouse, now in her early 40s. "Because I came of age before the reflowering of the women's movement in the early seventies, I have a certain distance from the corporate rat race and an ability to keep laughing at it. The main thing that has motivated me is doing challenging and stimulating work." It is such an attitude, Greenhouse says, that has enabled her to control her pace on the fast track.

When she was promoted to the newspaper's prestigious Washington, D.C., bureau in 1978, for instance, Greenhouse was wary of what she saw as the "onerous workaholic atmosphere" that lay before her. The standard thinking went something like this: For the privilege of working at the world's most respected newspaper in the world's most important city, reporters were expected to give their lives to the job. Those who got ahead routinely devoted themselves seven days a week, 24 hours a day, to their work. If reporters at the *Times* ever talked about finding time for themselves, it was in hushed tones, usually in a dark bar, and only then after several beers had numbed the senses. "Personal time," as one reporter put it, "just isn't part of the *Times*'s culture."

But Greenhouse knew that such blind devotion did not come without a price. She saw what it had done to her predecessor on the Supreme Court beat, who had burned out working seven days a week. Greenhouse couldn't see the logic of setting herself on the same destructive path. "I decided when I came to Washington that I was going to succeed on my terms. I said to myself that I would do this as a five-day-a-week job because that's what they're paying me to do. I may fail, but I'm going to fail trying to do it my way, which is preferable to ending up a burned-out basket case."

During more than a decade covering the Supreme Court beat, Greenhouse has rarely wavered from that promise she made to herself at the age of 31. She leaves the office every evening by 6 p.m., never works weekends and maintains a rewarding and successful career as a plateauer. Among her colleagues, the mere mention of Greenhouse's name provokes an extreme response: "No one could get away with what she has," says one. She's "brilliant," "amazing," insists another. But like my former colleague who managed a remarkable career himself as a writer for a national publication while working 40-hour weeks, Greenhouse's brilliance really has as much to do with setting limits and making choices as with any astonishing professional feats.

From the beginning, Greenhouse let it be known that she was not, in her words, "a one-person factory." Her predecessor had made it his responsibility to cover not only the highest legal body in the land but a variety of other courts and legal issues as well. Greenhouse, by contrast, has taken a far more focused approach to the beat. "I decided that with all the cases reaching the Supreme Court, no one could know everything. My strategy was just to do what I could and do it well." She has limited her coverage to the Supreme Court only and, the few times when she has been asked to take on other assignments, has refused to bend. "I have always put pretty defined limits on what I was willing to put up with."

By defining their limits, plateauers like Greenhouse set a pattern of behavior that becomes both expected and accepted by their employers. Furthermore, as in Greenhouse's case, their sensible approach to managing their careers enables them to do consistently superior work in a manner that is almost impossible for those who continually take on whatever is thrown their way. In the view of many of her colleagues, Greenhouse has paid a price for her independence by limiting her future advancement at the newspaper. In one sense, they are right. She has had to miss out on opportunities like covering the 1988 presidential campaign, and has essentially cut off the possibility of moving into management as an editor in the bureau. But Greenhouse could hardly be cast as deadwood. In fact, in 1990 she was one of 28 reporters and photographers awarded the new title of "senior journalist" for their distinguished careers at the newspaper. It was a vindication of sorts for Greenhouse, whose insistence on following her own course has not always come without a struggle.

At times, Greenhouse has found herself battling her own success—and sometimes ending up on the losing side. She faced just such a fight a few years ago when, after an eight-month maternity leave, she was moved from the Supreme Court beat to a plum assignment covering Congress with a handful of other reporters. It was a new challenge that allowed her to do longer analytical pieces and features while still maintaining a reasonable work schedule. But Greenhouse's reward for doing a superior job was a promotion she didn't particularly want. In January 1987, less than a year after switching to the new beat, her editors asked her to become the newspaper's chief congressional correspondent—rather than simply a member of the congressional reporting team. Greenhouse wasn't shy about expressing her reluctance to take the job. "I didn't really want to do it. I didn't feel very well prepared because the beat was still fairly new to me and I didn't know very much. I also didn't want to make that kind of commitment to be on call all the time to work weekends and get called at night. I told them I didn't want it."

Part of setting limits means recognizing that we do, in fact, have limitations. With less than a year's experience covering Congress, Greenhouse was honest enough with herself to realize that assuming the chief correspondent's role would require a monstrous commitment on her part. With a new baby and a new beat, Greenhouse knew that the additional responsibility was simply more than she wanted to take on at that point in her life. For Greenhouse, who almost habitually measures her personal priorities against her professional opportunities, the choice was obvious. Her editors, however, didn't see it that way. "The bureau chief really twisted my arm. He said, 'We understand your limitations. You'll have three people up there with you, just delegate. I understand what you are saying.'"

Greenhouse reluctantly agreed to take on the assignment, a decision she would later regret. "The understanding we supposedly had lasted about two months. Before long I was being asked to work weekends, and my editors got very annoyed when I wasn't around. I think they just assumed that in the competitive world in which we are all expected to live, I would simply rise to the occasion and mold myself to them. But I had made myself totally clear. I had no intention of doing that."

In this instance, Greenhouse did pay a short-term price for her insistence on setting limits: It was ultimately decided that she should step down from the beat. "My editors weren't going to leave me there on my terms and I wasn't going to change my life to meet their terms. It was not a very pleasant period. By a certain estimate I had failed—I hadn't measured up to what they expected. But I had never wanted to be the congressional bureau chief in the first place—I had been perfectly happy being part of a three-person bureau. Apparently that was something that just didn't make sense to them." For a short period after Greenhouse stopped covering Congress, she was assigned to a far less visible beat as legal analysis reporter but quickly returned to her old, comfortable stomping grounds at the Supreme Court.

Satisfied plateauers develop the ability to always grow and learn in whatever job they are doing—without requiring the external rewards of promotion to define their achievement. Although Greenhouse has covered the same beat for more than a decade, she feels challenged and rewarded by the process of thinking up new and innovative ways to approach similar stories. "I have tried to take advantage of changes in the newspaper in recent years to challenge myself to do more of the kind of writing that wasn't encouraged in the past, such as longer, more analytical pieces that are off the breaking news. As I have grown in the beat and come to understand the subject matter in more depth, I am more willing to take risks and experiment with new approaches to stories."

Of the five categories of downshifters I interviewed, the purposely plateaued like Greenhouse were typically the most independent and self-aware. They were the least inclined to allow their lives to be controlled by corporate game-playing or a traditional hierarchical mindset. Unlike back-trackers, whom you will meet in the next chapter, plateauers rarely sublimate their needs and values for a career or set themselves on a physically or emotionally destructive course before deciding to take a few steps down the ladder. As a result, they are rarely forced to downshift their careers to the extent of other dissatisfied career climbers. They also tend to maintain more outside involvements and interests than the typical professional, giving them a constant sense of balance and perspective even during the most stressful of times. Greenhouse, for instance, took Hebrew lessons for three years before her baby was born and pursued an interest in Mayan archeology, including making several trips to Central America.

Greenhouse has also not shied away from involvement in political and community issues, occasionally dropping her role as "objective reporter." When she marched for abortion rights in Washington, D.C., she drew criticism from colleagues and superiors at the newspaper who felt a journalist—especially one who covered the very issue in question—should not take such a public stand. The way Greenhouse saw it, however, expressing an opinion did not compromise her professional integrity any more than leaving the office by 6 p.m. or turning down a promotion and acknowledging that she did, in fact, have a personal life. "My role as a reporter for the *New York Times* is just one part of who I am," she says. "I can't allow it to control me."

The "exciting" fast track versus the "boring" slow track

The sense of self so many of us search for through a career is, ironically, illusory, if we allow our lives to be controlled by our employers and our identities to be defined by the job. If we give our careers such power, are we really so different than the organization man who at the whim of the corporation packed up his family and made yet another cross-country transfer?

What we fear more than anything else is boredom—or, more aptly, being boring. We are forever fighting that image in our heads of devoted, responsible moms and dads who unquestioningly acted out their comfortable middle-class roles. We insist that what we are creating for ourselves is superior—and in some ways, it is. Both women and men clearly have more choices than they did a generation ago. But in our pursuit of exciting careers and insistence on avoiding "boring" lives, we too easily limit our choices and give up what matters most: the sense of family and community that defined our parents' world.

For many plateauers, reinventing success means redefining long-held ideas about what constitutes a dull and uninspiring life versus an "exciting" one. Take Michael Johnson. At first glance, he is not the sort of professional we are taught to emulate. For the past 16 years, Johnson has purposely and strategically maintained a slow-track career as a hydrogeologist with the U.S. Geological Survey after giving up a high-paying, fast-track job with Shell Oil. His income has lingered at about the $40,000 mark, and Johnson lives modestly with his wife, Jolena, a substitute schoolteacher, and their three daughters in a four-bedroom house in Carson City, Nevada, 30 miles outside of Lake Tahoe.

On the surface, Johnson's life is the embodiment of the secure predictability that exemplified the organization man's unchanging existence, with none of the thrills and challenges that typify the world of the career climber. What makes Johnson different—and special—however, is that unlike either the organization man or the career climber, he has successfully controlled his own destiny. His relatively low-key life is far more rewarding than the one he tasted many years ago as a hotshot in the oil industry. Says Johnson, who is now in his early 40s: "When I was younger, I just went with the flow like everyone else. I allowed my career to zoom ahead with no plan for how it would fit into the rest of my life." But unlike many career climbers, Johnson saw quickly that his successful, exciting career was making him miserable.

It was the late sixties, and Johnson was fresh out of school with an honors degree in physics from Portland State University. He had been an outstanding student with a 3.7 grade point average in his major and a 4.0 in math, and had his pick of a wide range of promising professional paths. He opted for a position as a geophysicist with Shell Oil. After only a few years, he was heading a 54-person crew searching for oil and gas. His star was rising quickly and the rewards were enticing. "The money was great and there were a lot of opportunities for upward advancement," Johnson recalls.

But it was also a period of profound soul-searching and self-discovery for Johnson. A common characteristic of plateauers is to start such questioning early on in their careers. "When I was first starting out, like everyone else, I looked to other people's experiences to guide me and give me some context for how I should live my life because at that point I had so little understanding of my own preferences. It was when I finally got the courage to act on my own experiences and needs that I could think about alternatives."

In his field, being guided by "other people's experiences" meant blindly following the corporate directive. "I moved where they wanted me to move and jumped when they wanted me to jump." During his five and a half years at Shell, Johnson was transferred six times. Just as he would start to establish roots and begin to feel a sense of belonging, the corporate dictum would come down again telling him to pack his bags and start the cycle all over. "It was almost a given, an unwritten rule, that you would go where the company said you would go, or you wouldn't have a job," recalls Johnson.

Increasingly, professionals are rebelling against such attitudes. In a 1988 study of 2,000 Mobil Oil Corporation employees, 27 percent of the men surveyed and 19 percent of the women had turned down transfers in the previous five years. In more than half those cases, the transfer would have involved a promotion. The company estimated that the overall rate of employee relocation refusals could climb to as high as 39 percent in the next ten years as two-career couples, in particular, become less willing to uproot their families and their lives for the corporation. "Ten years ago, relocation refusals were very much the exception. There was a sense that you didn't dare refuse to move or it would seriously hurt your career," says Jean Baderschneider, an employee relations manager for Mobil. "Today, so many people are doing it that the attitudes, out of necessity, have had to change."

Most surprising, however, is who is doing it. According to the Mobil study, white males over 35 were by far the most resistant to relocation. As one Mobil executive who turned down a transfer put it: "I wanted the kids to have a place they could call home. Up to this point, with all the relocating I've had to do, they really haven't." Women under 35, along with their male counterparts, were also inclined to refuse to relocate and placed a high emphasis on family concerns.

By contrast, the typical professional woman over 35, unlike Greenhouse, was the most willing to uproot herself for her career at Mobil and was the least likely to be concerned with family issues. This group was generally single and almost always childless—only 10 percent had children. "These women had clearly given up family for career and were ready to go wherever the company wanted them to," says Baderschneider.

My interviews, however, revealed a decidedly changing

picture for women in this category. More than perhaps any of the other career climbers I spoke with, they were painfully aware of the sacrifices they had made to prove themselves professionally. Without exception, they were now attempting to pull back and make time for themselves and relationships beyond work. For the first time in their adult lives, they were talking about marriage, thinking about starting families late in life, and making conscious efforts to downplay their careers. As one computer industry executive in her late 30s put it: "There is nothing more exciting and worthwhile that I could think of doing with my life right now than settling down. I used to think transfers were exciting because I could experience living in different parts of the country. But after eight moves in fifteen years, I've had enough."

It took Michael Johnson considerably less time to decide that he had had enough. Johnson had always valued the sense of closeness and stability found in smalltown life, but he had chosen a career that directly worked against those things. "Geographic fulfillment," as Johnson puts it, was an integral part of his success imagery. "I was raised in Oregon and feel most at home in the western United States. I like going from the forests and spruce trees to the coast. I loved the work I was doing at Shell, but moving ahead there would have meant always relocating and never really belonging to a community."

Like Deschere and Greenhouse, Johnson finds inherent value in his work and has little trouble coming up with new ways to keep himself challenged—with or without the external rewards provided by promotions. He is endlessly fascinated with the technical aspects of his profession and, if left to his own devices, will rattle on for hours about the intricacies of electromagnetic radiation or wave theory. Such passion is typical of plateauers, who are often found in creative or technically oriented fields. On the other hand, downshifting professionals whose strengths and interests lie in management may find a more compatible fit as a career shifter (Chapter 5) or self-employer (Chapter 6), which typically provide more opportunities to grow in leadership or organizational roles.

Johnson knew he could find ways to feel satisfied in a job that allowed him to stay close to the scientific aspects of his field. "At Shell, the pressure would always have been on to accept transfers and move into managerial jobs," says Johnson. In order to keep his career on a steady course it would first be necessary for Johnson to make a career shift into an environment that was inherently more open to a slower track. In 1974, he took a 34 percent pay cut and went to work for the U.S. Geological Survey, a government job that offers more stability and puts less emphasis on relocating. He has spent much of the past two decades examining groundwater supplies and coming up with new methods of tapping potential water sources. His passion for his work is still remarkably strong. When I first interviewed Johnson he was full of stories about an experiment he had just conducted in the middle of the night to test the water supply at a nearby country club. "It was a lot of fun," he beamed. "A touch of exploration, science and intrigue. It was really neat."

Johnson, however, is less enthusiastic about the economic tradeoffs he has made. In the 20 years he has been in the earth sciences field, his salary has increased an average of about 1 percent a year. "When I was at Shell, I got two paychecks a month and could throw one in the desk and live off the other." But he has turned down offers to move into higher-level management jobs in the government because they would have forced him to relocate, and sees advantages to the plateaued lifestyle. Unlike his career-climbing counterparts, he does not feel the pressures of having to keep up with an upwardly mobile lifestyle. By staying put in the highly affordable community of Carson City, for instance, he and his wife have been able to maintain a stable lifestyle for their children and not worry about fluctuations in the real-estate market that have created problems for fast-track transferees in recent years. Friends who stuck with the corporate path say they are envious of Johnson, despite their higher incomes. "They have told me that they wished they had made the move earlier on, but that now they feel it is too late. They feel trapped by their bigger salaries."

Many professionals almost routinely accept that feeling of being trapped as an inevitable price of career success. Plateauers, as we have seen, refuse to do so. They learn early on the value of taking charge of their professional paths and form a success mindset that keeps them on a steady course—no matter how intense the external pressures.

Most of us, however, routinely define our personal success according to the expectations of others. Choosing to do otherwise, as plateauers have, will not come naturally for the majority of career climbers who have relied on societal standards to show them the way to a successful life. Particularly for those who have measured their success along an accelerated fast track, the process of assuming control and gaining the type of balance perfected by the plateauer will, at the very least, be an uncomfortable journey. It may even be a painful one. But as we will see in the following chapter, the process of moving down the ladder a notch or two can ultimately be a more exhilarating trip than continuing the endless race upward.

4

· ·

The Back-Tracker

If there is one given about a successful career path, it is that we travel up, not down. Advice books urge us to keep our eye on the next rung of the ladder, follow in the footsteps of those who have made it to the top, and always, *always* aim higher. We are conditioned to the idea of achieving one goal, and then, almost by rote, moving on to the next. Particularly for professionals whose careers have been highly accelerated, stepping back and considering other options may come only after several years of traveling upward and moving further away from where they want to be.

In a particularly ironic fallout of the fast-track eighties, a growing number of professionals I interviewed were looking to correct their missteps by, in some cases, taking dramatic leaps backwards. The words of one hotel industry executive echoed the concerns of many of these disillusioned career climbers: "I keep thinking that if I could just go back to where I was seven years ago I would be a lot happier. But I wouldn't know where to begin. The income cut is the least of my concerns. I'm just worried that people would think I was crazy."

Unlike plateauers, this group's images of success are drawn heavily from parental and societal expectations rather than their own internal notions of achievement. But as we have seen, many baby boomer professionals have misinterpreted the 1950s parental notion of success or have embraced only one part of it—the part that equated success with moving upward in a career, not with having a strong and supportive family and community life. Because they have focused so heavily on career success, moving backwards is a particularly unsettling prospect. Some dismiss the notion outright. They may, instead, choose the "dropout" role, shoving the professions they love out of their lives completely rather than confronting their dissatisfaction head-on. Or they may absorb themselves with fantasies of how it used to be, imagining that life would be better if, like the young executive in the Kellogg's commercial, they could snap their fingers and wake up in an idealized world of nine-to-five bliss. In the past, however, few dared to take a realistic, strategic step backwards. As the hotel executive put it: "Going backwards would feel like failure. I would probably be happier, but I couldn't do it because I'd be too consumed by the idea that I was a failure. It would be easier to just quit completely."

Getting over the idea that they will be cast as failures is the greatest challenge facing career back-trackers. For females, for example, who have climbed to a position of authority in male-dominated fields, the thought of abruptly stepping backward seems to legitimize the stereotype that women don't have what it takes to make it at the top. Deborah Coleman of Apple carried on her shoulders the enormous responsibility of being a role model for hundreds of young women. When she decided to cut back in 1989 and move into a lesser job as a vice-president of the company, many of her followers felt let down. "I think she ruined her career and hurt all women in Silicon Valley," said one former colleague. Coleman was well aware of her detractors. "I know that some women thought, 'Oh my god, here's the highest-ranking woman in Silicon Valley and she's voluntarily stepping back; she must have caved in to the pressure.' "

In fact, for men and women alike, stepping back is frequently the culmination of a painful battle between personal needs and professional expectations. In the competitive world of masculine achievement, back-tracking is often viewed as copping out. "Everyone's immediate reaction was to assume that I was getting lazy," recalls Steve Garagiola, who gave up a top sports anchor job with a Detroit television station to go to work for a far smaller station in Phoenix with lower pay and more flexible hours. "People seemed to think that I just wanted to kick back, play golf and get in the comfort zone." As Garagiola knew all too well, however, making such a move is anything but comfortable. "Believe me, it is not comfortable to throw your life into the air and see how many pieces it breaks into."

Yet, for some professionals, it is often the only way to get their careers—and lives—back on track. In many instances, as we will see in this chapter, the glamour and power of their jobs become all-consuming, pushing them away from their families and sense of identity. In their effort to "fit in" and meet the expectations of their bosses and colleagues, they often lose track of themselves. Recalls Ray Everngam: "I had submerged myself so completely in my professional identity that there were times when *I* didn't even know who I was anymore." Many in this group have bought into the belief that work can provide it all—a sense of community, family and meaning—only to realize that their complete career immersion has left them with none of those.

Fighting the glamour trap

Much of our thinking and expectations about modern careers come from our notion of a glamour job. Certain professions, such as entertainment, journalism, advertising and law, make for great television scripts. The Hollywood imagery, rather than the substantive work itself, may even trigger our initial interest in a particular career. A surge in law school applications during the late 1980s, for instance, was attributed in large part to the popularity of the television show "L.A. Law." It's a good bet that many of those applicants were more attracted to the designer clothes and glamorous lifestyles of the tv litigators than the prospects of poring through piles of legal documents in windowless warehouses.

But such imagery doesn't only influence our career choices. It contributes to an overall impression of what constitutes a successful life. We have made it when our expense account and exclusive address reflect the part. In some professions, the perks we are awarded for each step up the ladder may even matter more than the actual salaries we take home. First-class airline travel, door-to-door limo service and an executive health club membership scream to the world that we belong to the professional elite.

The job description of a television journalist implicitly includes a well-groomed, stylish appearance. An advertising account executive who hasn't mastered the art of the expense account client lunch in unlikely to get the big business and move ahead in the organization. By their very nature, however, glamour careers support values that run counter to building a happy and healthy family life. As Steve Garagiola says: "It's very easy to let your whole being get caught up in your professional identity because the work is so much fun and you are getting all this recognition. When I was in Detroit, I was a big shot. Everywhere I went, people would come up to me, want to shake my hand and talk about the Tigers. With all of that around you, it's easy to forget there is anything else."

From the day he entered the television business, Garagiola had worked hard to resist falling into the glamour trap. As the son of former professional athlete and tv sports personality Joe Garagiola, he was intimately aware of the reality behind the glossy images. "My father worked very hard to try to make us a family and I think he succeeded. But he had regrets about being on the road so much when we were growing up. He was always up front with me about the negative side of this business."

Garagiola approached his decision to follow in his father's professional footsteps with a clearsighted perspective that he felt certain would allow him to be successful in the field he loved and still keep his life in balance. But, like many back-trackers, Garagiola's meteoric rise started to control him at an age when he felt powerless to resist. For many career climbers, the rush of excitement that accompanies instant success can be addictive, like a drug. In the midst of such professional highs, setting limits and saying "no" seems impossible. "You feel like you don't need anything else because there is this constant adrenaline rush. You feel like you are in total control—like you could do anything," recalls Matthew Simon, the young real-estate tycoon who fell victim to chronic fatigue syndrome.

Garagiola's career, like Simon's, was headed for the stratosphere before he had time to catch his breath. Following a two-and-a-half-year stint after college at a small station in Lansing, Michigan, Garagiola jumped from the ninety-eighth biggest television market in the country to number seven. He was 26 years old. For two years, he was a reporter and weekend sports anchor for

WXYZ in Detroit. But Garagiola, who was just starting a family with his wife, Carol, an attorney, was determined to keep his career in perspective. His relatively modest goal was to someday anchor the 6 o'clock weekday sportscast—a job that would allow him to continue reporting in the field while keeping his evenings free to spend with his family. Garagiola, however, turned out to be too good for his own good. He was offered something "better."

Two years after Garagiola's arrival at WXYZ, the station's two top sports anchors left. Suddenly there were vacancies to fill, and Garagiola was waiting in the wings. He was asked to take over the 5 and 11 o'clock weekday shows. "Even then I knew what I really wanted was to just do the six o'clock so that I could have a normal life. But it was an offer I couldn't refuse," he says. A few years later, Garagiola was presented with yet another so-called opportunity—the 6 o'clock newscast. "They presented it like this would make me *the* sports guy for the station. I didn't think I could say no," says Garagiola.

Professionals who decide to backtrack frequently get caught in similar success cycles. Many of the back-trackers I interviewed characterized their initial success as "unexpected," often the result of "good timing" or a "quirk of fate" that landed them coveted positions five or even ten years before they had anticipated. One of the inherent flaws of the fast track is that it pushes young careerists into roles that they may not be prepared to handle, either emotionally or professionally. Still, as a culture, we continue to glorify those who move up the quickest. As one former fast-tracker put it: "It's the under-thirty rule. If you can get there before you're thirty years old, you are a certifiable whiz kid. Never mind the fact that you haven't had time to think about what you're doing, learn from your mistakes and become a mature, well-rounded person. By society's definition you are a success."

Even for those who may question where their speedy

climb is really taking them and, like Garagiola, would prefer a slower track, the constant societal encouragement leads young fast-trackers to buy into the idea that they should feel happy and privileged with their astounding success. Recalls Garagiola: "Every time I would express my doubts to colleagues or friends, they would say things like, 'There are a million people out there who would kill their grandmothers to do what you're doing. What do you have to complain about?' So I would just push aside my doubts and keep going."

Before long, however, the stress of handling three shows a day and never getting home before 12:30 in the morning began to take a serious toll on Garagiola's family life. His marriage disintegrated to the point where he and Carol were little more than two babysitters trading shifts. Carol, who was doing legal work part-time, would come home at midday and take over baby-sitting duties from Garagiola, who then took off for the station. "In terms of a relationship it was ridiculous," says Garagiola. "We knew each other, but that was it." Although the morning hours at home gave Garagiola time to spend with his youngest daughter, Megan, he had become a virtual stranger to Katie, who was off at school often before he was able to rouse himself and would be asleep by the time he got home. It was, in fact, a particularly hurtful comment expressed by then 8-year-old Katie that forced Garagiola to start honestly assessing where his superstar lifestyle was leading him. "Sometimes I feel like I don't even have a daddy," Katie cried to her mother one evening while Garagiola was at work.

Although he had vowed never to let it happen to him, Garagiola's career had taken control of his life. It was his daughter's heartfelt words that brought him back to reality and forced him to start realigning his personal values with his public persona. "What she said really broke my heart because I knew it was true," says Garagiola. "I was doing the best I thought I could under the circumstances. But I would get home at twelve-thirty in the morning and then not be able to fall asleep until two-thirty because I was so buzzed from doing the late show. I would try to get up as many mornings as I could at six for breakfast before Katie went off to school and try to visit with her for a few minutes before going back to bed, but it wasn't a relationship. It was stupid. It was nothing."

As the painful possibility of divorce became more and more of a reality, Garagiola took a hard look at the life he had built for himself and decided the thrill of being a top sports anchor in Detroit wasn't worth throwing away his family. He began taking steps to put his career in reverse.

Garagiola's initial plan was to try to work out a new schedule with the Detroit station. But stepping backwards within an organization where one has been cast in a high-profile role is often a messy process. In most cases, backtracking is best accomplished by switching to a different department or separate area within a department or, as Garagiola found, moving to another organization altogether. In some fields, where such moves are especially taboo, making a career shift to a related position may prove more realistic and rewarding, as will be discussed in Chapter 5. In highly competitive fields, in particular, maintaining control of one's career means setting limits early on—as Linda Greenhouse did. Unlike Greenhouse, however, Garagiola had never established a pattern of saying "no." To the contrary, station management had come to expect his complete and total devotion to the job.

As a result, when Garagiola presented his plan to be taken off the 5 and 11 o'clock newscasts and work as an anchor on the 6 o'clock show only, his superiors, in Garagiola's words, "thought it was weird. As far as they knew, they had never heard of anyone, anyplace who had *asked* to be taken off the 11 o'clock show. It was the primo spot." When station management came back with a response, it was clear to Garagiola that they did not see a place for him if he wasn't willing to play according to their rules. Their "non-negotiable" 90-day contract called for Garagiola to do the 6 o'clock weekday shows, as well as Sunday newscasts, and to take a 50 percent pay cut. "It was obvious to me that they didn't see this working out. If I didn't want to do tv the way they felt it was done, I was just going to fade into the background." Garagiola felt he had no choice. He left without a job.

The weeks after Garagiola made the decision to backtrack and then quit without another offer were among the most stressful of his career. The problem for many back-trackers is that by the time they decide to make a change, they are emotionally already near the end of their rope. Many may have driven themselves to physical exhaustion and even serious illness, as Matthew Simon did. Almost all are likely to have experienced some symptoms of emotional burnout or a personal crisis that ultimately forces them to take action. "When I started to take things apart professionally, I was probably at an emotional low," says Garagiola. "My family and marriage were already in trouble and to save that I had to throw the cards in the air professionally."

Beyond his own internal struggles, Garagiola also had to deal with the reactions of colleagues and friends who couldn't understand why he seemed to be throwing away a dream job. The day the memo went up in the newsroom announcing his departure, Garagiola's colleagues initially assumed he was headed to New York for a network assignment. "When I told them I was just going home, that I didn't have another offer, they couldn't believe it. People couldn't imagine why I had done this. Here I was with this great job. I was a big shot in a top-ten market with a six-figure salary. The station was thrilled with the way things had been going with me. If I had just gone in and said, 'Let's sign another three-year contract,' there would have been no problem. I brought the roof down on myself."

Despite the occasional feelings of self-doubt and the sus-
pecting, noncomprehending comments from others, what made
all the difference for Garagiola was that he had made the decision
himself—he had said "no." For the first time in his meteoric
career, he had taken control of his life. "I had this real sense of
confidence because I knew it was the right thing to do. I knew that
if I kept doing what I was doing for another year, I would be
divorced and wouldn't have a family anymore. Is that enough for
me? No way, it isn't even close. It's ridiculous. I had to keep giving
myself pep talks that it was going to work out."

After leaving WXYZ, Garagiola was offered several similar
positions in big markets with high salaries. He turned them all
down to accept a job as a sports anchor for the 5 p.m. newscast
on KTSP-TV in Phoenix. It is a job with far less responsibility and
prestige, in a smaller market, at a smaller station. A year into the
new position, Garagiola's salary was in the five-figure range instead of six-figure. In Detroit, he was only a few steps away from
a network spot. He is now several steps away. The white stucco
home Garagiola and his wife bought in Scottsdale is not as big as
the brick colonial they had back in suburban Detroit. But it has
a pool and small Jacuzzi, and Garagiola is home every evening
to enjoy his new life with his wife and daughters. "I'll come home
and they'll be out in the back and Megan will yell, "It's Daddy!"
They'll come charging up to me, tugging at me to come into the
pool. I feel now that I'm part of what they're doing—I'm part of
putting them to bed, part of homework, part of their lives. That's
what it's all about."

What's more, Garagiola, like many back-trackers, has
found greater professional contentment down the ladder. In fact,
having risen quickly and then dropped back has given him a rare
ability to call his own shots at an age when many people would
still be scrambling to get ahead. As a result, his less glamorous
position is fuller and more satisfying than his high-profile job in

Detroit. "I don't have to be on the air three times a day, sitting behind a desk and reading sports scores. I have more time and flexibility to do the kind of work I love, which is producing, editing and making television, not just being on television." Much of his job now consists of tracking down and developing human interest stories, such as a feature on jockeys in the Kentucky Derby. "I was able to spend time interviewing them about what it really feels like to be riding in the biggest race—what is in their hearts. Doing stories like that is what makes this business so much fun."

Because he has already experienced the fast track, Garagiola says he no longer feels compelled to set new career goals for himself that would move him up the professional ladder again. "I got that out of my system. Now I just feel this great sense of freedom. I don't have to worry about moving up to the next biggest market. I can concentrate, instead, on doing rewarding work and enjoying my life."

When careers smother our identities

As Garagiola found, when the goal of moving up in a career takes over, sometimes it's easy to lose track of why we were drawn to a particular profession in the first place. Perhaps even more troubling, when we confine our goals to the expectations and values of a singular success track, we may end up forcing our very identities into an ill-fitting mold. Many of us have looked to our careers to provide us with a sense of identity. Ironically, what we are finding, instead, is that the demands and standards of those careers end up chipping away at who we really are.

More than perhaps any of the other professionals you will meet in this book, back-trackers have relied heavily on the external rules of success to define them. In many cases, they have been influenced by a 1950s-era parental voice that seemed to insist success meant making more money and being more successful in a career than they had been. While these professionals have internalized that parental voice, they have never fully accepted it. Many, in fact, are consumed by a desire to be different in every way from their parents. Consider the story of Ray Everngam.

When I first met Everngam, I was struck by his quiet, thoughtful manner and dry wit. From what I knew of him, from how he had in fact described himself over the phone, I pictured a professional whose frenetic impatience and drive would literally burst the buttons of his Oxford shirt and bust the seams of his navy blazer. Instead, Everngam displayed a soft-spoken intelligence and creativity that seemed far removed from the fast-track imagery. His words naturally transformed themselves into metaphor. He punctuated his speech with references to literature and mythology. One thing was obvious: Ray Everngam was no sterotypical career climber.

Yet, for much of the past decade, that was exactly the role he had played. "For a while," he says, "I fooled a lot of people. Even myself." Just a few months earlier he had given up the act, stepping down from his position as editorial manager of journals and books for the 120,000-member National Association of Social Workers and purposely planting himself several steps down the ladder as a production specialist with no management responsibilities for the American Chemical Society. He had also taken a $10,000 paycut.

But the decision did not come without a struggle for Everngam, who had always believed success meant one thing. As he puts it: "If you climbed a professional ladder and made more money you were successful. If you didn't you were a failure." Everngam's vision of success was derived, in large part, from his tradition-minded parents. His father, a government bureaucrat who worked in essentially the same job for several decades, and his mother, who longed for a lawyer son with a six-figure income, long ago had set for Everngam the terms of a successful life. When he went to work as a proofreader for *National Geographic* after college, to pursue an interest in writing and publishing, it was not exactly what they had in mind. But Everngam was determined to make up for his "untraditional career choice" by moving up as quickly as possible in his chosen field. "I felt this pressure to rapidly prove that I could make something of myself even if I wasn't doing exactly what I was 'supposed' to be doing," he says.

In quick succession, Everngam moved from *National Geographic* to a position with the National Academy of Sciences, where he refined his editing and production skills working on several of the organization's international journals, and then on to the Entomological Society of America, where he was handed his first major position of responsibility as managing editor of all publications for the organization. The unassuming 10,000-member association was the perfect place for Everngam to apply his budding creative and managerial skills. "When I first arrived there were no real procedures in place for producing the journals and magazines. I organized the whole thing and expanded several publications. It was great. I made the decisions, played an active role in implementing them and then watched it all fall into place," he says. The job's relatively predictable hours also gave Everngam time to pursue a range of eclectic interests outside of work, from writing fiction to gardening to working on a master's in political science.

Everngam's long-held image of career success, however, was still influenced by his parents' notion that "bigger is better." For Everngam that meant moving on to a larger, more prestigious organization where his success would be more readily apparent to the outside world. His next stop was the huge National Association of Social Workers, where, at least by conventional standards, his career took off. "I was promoted twice in six months and my salary kept going up. It was exciting. I felt successful." But as Everngam's successes grew, so did his responsibilities. Before long, his job had expanded far beyond his talent for overseeing the publication of books and journals. He spent long hours drawing up departmental budgets, working on long-term strategic planning for the organization and even negotiating with unhappy union employees. "I didn't have the background and experience, let alone the interest, for any of this," recalls Everngam.

It was also becoming increasingly clear to Everngam that his easygoing personality and playful sense of humor were not suited to the conservative, rigid world of big organization management. "I was literally reprimanded for being funny, for doing these really innocent practical jokes." One day, when a sink overflowed in the office kitchen, Everngam decided to ease office tension by adding a humorous touch to the mishap: He placed a few sheets of whale-shaped paper from the senior editor's memo pad on the puddle of water. The lighthearted stunt brought harsh words from his supervisor. "What I had done was completely harmless. But I got a memo from him saying managers don't act that way," says Everngam. "There was a whole ethic and code of behavior that wasn't me. But I was forcing myself to fit into it."

Most of us accept career conformity as an unavoidable tradeoff of professionalism. From the type of clothes we wear when playing our professional roles to the food we order while dining with clients, the pressures to conform affect all of us to varying degrees. The problem comes when relatively minor tradeoffs in taste and interests become massive obstacles to personal fulfillment and individual expression. Women who believe they must "be like men" in order to gain acceptance into the good-old-boy hierarchy are frequently victims of this type of career conformity. Carol Bartz, vice-president of worldwide field operations for Sun Microsystems, went so far as to cover up her pregnancy for six months. "I wore double-breasted blazers and used a lot of safety pins—no one had a clue. I would be visiting army bases in the middle of the desert where it was boiling hot and I would be wearing these big jackets. That's how crazy I was. I was so afraid that people would think less of me, that they would think I had softened and wasn't tough enough to be in the kind of position I was in."

In Everngam's case the pressures to mold himself to an ill-fitting professional role began pulling him away from his friends and interests beyond work. Slowly, as he describes it, he started "shedding pieces of himself." He stopped writing fiction. He shoved aside the master's in political science that he had been working toward. He stopped calling friends and family. He never got around to paying the bills. "I put everything outside of work on indefinite hold," remembers Everngam, who is single and in his mid-30s. "All my commitments had to be focused on work because it required so much energy just to keep it going. Paying bills, talking to people, it was just too much of a hassle and I couldn't deal with any outside hassles."

Like other back-trackers, however, Everngam's dissatisfaction alone was not enough to spur him to make a change. Instead, the turning point came when he realized his job stress was having a serious impact on his physical and mental well-being. Everngam started to have what he describes as "panic attacks," in which he would hyperventilate and feel as if he were having a heart attack. "I felt I was approaching the end of my rope. It was just a matter of time before all this stress that was building up inside of me resulted in a serious car accident, major illness or complete nervous breakdown.' "

Everngam reached near-total collapse before he stopped

ignoring his unhappiness and started thinking about what he needed to do to lead a healthy, balanced life. He had to look seven or eight years into the past and three giant notches down the ladder. It was there that he saw a person he recognized and liked; a person who enjoyed his work and his life and hadn't given up so much of himself for a career he found increasingly dissatisfying.

Within a few months, Everngam accepted a job as a production specialist for the American Chemical Society in Washington, D.C. Although his salary was cut by $10,000, he was back doing work he enjoyed, without the political pressures of other executive responsibilities. While making the actual job switch proved relatively simple, Everngam's self-demotion was far from painless. For starters, he found it more difficult than he had anticipated to push aside his managerial role and quietly accept subordination. Within only a few weeks after starting the job, Everngam was already fighting the urge to reassert his old authority and tell superiors that there might be a better way to get the job done. The large salary cut also weighed heavily on both Everngam's ego and lifestyle. Despite preparing himself ahead of time and building up a savings cushion, he found it impossible to maintain his old standard of living with a $10,000 loss in income. In addition to forgoing expensive dining out and buying less clothing, Everngam also had to worry for the first time in years about whether he could meet monthly car and mortgage payments.

Everngam began to think that in his desperation to make a change he had perhaps taken too drastic a leap backwards. About six months into his new job, however, the problem resolved itself. Everngam received a call from his old employer, the Entomological Society of America, which was looking for a managing editor of books and journals—the very position he had left several years before. The job offered an ideal mix of managerial and creative tasks and was a position Everngam knew he felt comfortable in. "For me, the idea of going back to a job I had been promoted out of would have been totally absurd a few years ago. I wouldn't have even considered it. But now it made perfect sense. It was exactly what I wanted."

Like Garagiola, Everngam discovered that his experience with a larger organization gave him the leverage to create new opportunities for himself within his old position, including negotiating a salary that was only $2,000 less than his income at the National Association of Social Workers. He also found that he now had the clout and the confidence to push his department in new directions, including implementing a variety of innovative high-tech production systems. "I find the technology end of publishing fascinating. It is a whole new area I can excel in."

Maintaining the sense of balance achieved through backtracking is, of course, the toughest challenge faced by people like Everngam. Those who pull it off adopt the success system of plateauers. They learn to value the internal challenges of professional success rather than rely on such external rewards as promotions. Because they have already proven to themselves—and the outside world—that they have what it takes to climb quickly in a career, they can now search out new areas for measuring their achievements. Many come to see themselves as lifelong students who gain satisfaction from developing their understanding of a particular concept or technology.

George Mais backtracked his career as a manager of software systems for New York Telephone Company (now NYNEX Corporation) several years ago when he grew frustrated with the political infighting and endless meetings that dominated his supervisory role. For nearly a decade since then, he has held the same job as an in-house software consultant, with no staff or managerial responsibilities. But Mais, who had always preferred the technical side of the business, feels more challenged today than during those years when he was being handed regular promotions into the management ranks. "I am always expanding my knowledge by doing outside reading and taking courses to learn about new technologies. I enjoy more than anything else the process of learning new things and passing that knowledge on to others."

Without the daily pressures to conform to a role he was ill-suited to play, Everngam discovered that he could be both successful in a career and true to himself. He now sees that his natural curiosity and wide range of interests beyond work could never be satisfied by the fast track. These days, Everngam's revised success imagery includes writing a novel "just for the fun of it," working with the town council of his community of Washington Grove, Maryland, to landscape overgrown parkland areas throughout the town, and reacquainting himself with friends and family he had pushed out of his life when the demands of his career closed in. "It's like I had put all of these hunks of myself into boxes and I was just storing them in the back of my mind, waiting for retirement so I could open them up again. Right now, I feel like it's Christmas. I'm opening all these boxes and rediscovering these whole pieces of myself that I had lost. It's amazing how far I had drifted from the values I originally set out with after college. I feel like I'm becoming a whole person again."

Breaking free of the "community of work"

When we spend 60, 70 or 80 hours a week at the office, when our intellectual and social energies are so focused on our careers that we barely have time to read a book or call a friend, it's easy, as we have seen, to lose our emotional bearings. In Everngam's case the result was a gradual drifting away from a sense of self.

Others may find themselves becoming increasingly detached from the larger community outside of work—from not only friends and family but from a sense of belonging to and participating in a world beyond day-to-day career concerns.

Instead, work becomes both our community and our family. The corporate culture, with its clear mission and purpose, offers a sense of direction and security as we try to establish our own professional and personal identities. The chief executive's passion to build "the greatest company in the world" and create the best product or service becomes the driving force in the lives of eager professionals as well. As we saw in Chapter 2, the pressures on today's managers to produce more and put in longer hours makes it especially difficult to separate ourselves from the community of work. The message is that if we pull back we'll let the team down and splinter the tight-knit corporate family. Those of us who aren't willing to run the race like everyone else may be viewed as lacking devotion and commitment.

Such attitudes are especially pervasive in many of today's so-called enlightened corporate cultures, where the emphasis on family and community often seems to be a gentler way of encouraging workaholism and career tunnel vision. It's easy to get swept away by the vitality and surface exuberance of such organizations, where young upstarts may find themselves sharing meals in the company cafeteria with the CEO and being asked on a whim to take part in the development of the "fastest," "most innovative," "most remarkable" (choose your superlative) computer, telecommunications system, theme park or health food product ever invented. When Wendy Osborn Stenzel came to Tandem Computer in the late 1970s, she happily immersed herself in just such a culture. "We all believed that if we worked hard we could do absolutely anything," she says. "We were driven to produce the best product—in this case, a computer that could not go down. There was this feeling that we could always come up with the best ideas and execute them better than anyone else. We were a family. We were in it together."

In such an atmosphere, incredible demands and absurdly long hours are not seen as burdens. Rather, they are challenges to be met and conquered. As Tracy Kidder depicted in his book *The Soul of a New Machine,* such work environments attract bright, impressionable professionals anxious to prove they have the right stuff. Consider Kidder's account of recruitment efforts at Data General Corporation, which was assembling a team of young engineers to build, in record speed, the company's next generation of minicomputers:

> "It's gonna be tough," says the project recruiter. "If we hired you, you'd be working with a bunch of cynics and egotists and it'd be hard to keep up with them."
>
> "That doesn't scare me," replies the recruit.
>
> "There's a lot of fast people in this group. . . . It's gonna be a real hard job with a lot of long hours. And I mean *long* hours."
>
> "No," says the recruit, "that's what I want to do, get in on the ground floor of a new architecture. I want to do a big machine. I want to be where the action is."
>
> "Well, we can only let in the best of this year's graduates. We've already let in some awfully fast people. We'll have to let you know.
>
> "We tell him that we only let in the best. Then we let him in.
>
> "I don't know," says the project recruiter afterwards. "It was kind of like recruiting for a

suicide mission. You're gonna die. But you're gonna die in glory."[1]

Since *The Soul of a New Machine* was published in 1981, much has changed in the high-stakes world of computer manufacturing. Many companies—such as Data General, which has made massive layoffs and lost its industry prominence—found that the "do it all, do it now" philosophy only speeded their fall into financial hardship. For those eager recruits at Data General as well, the rewards turned out to be disappointing. Although they succeeded in building a new machine, they paid an enormous price. Many were emotionally and physically burned out and left the company. Marriages and personal lives were destroyed, and several team members vowed "never again."[2]

The absorption in work demanded by such corporate cultures, while intoxicating and exciting, inherently shuts out almost everything else. By their very ideology, these elite clubs— these communities of work—exclude the existence of and participation in an outside family or community. Ironically, members tend to speak of their commitment with a fervor that echoes the passions of the anitwar and civil rights activists of the 1960s. "We had this idea that if we worked hard enough we could really make a difference," recalls Wendy Osborn Stenzel, whose career in graphic design took off in the late 1970s when she joined Tandem Computer, then a fast-growing computer industry upstart headed by the charismatic visionary Jim Treybig. At Tandem, however, "making a difference" didn't mean "changing the world" as it had for those idealistic sixties activists. It meant "creating the best product before anyone else did," says Stenzel.

When Stenzel was accepted into this dynamic community after graduating from college, it offered the sense of both security and purpose she was searching for following the death of her father from cancer. Stenzel had set off for California from her hometown of Austin, Texas, intent on putting her degree in graphic design to use and "doing something meaningful with my life. I had a real sense of mortality after my father's death. I felt this incredible need to make something of myself quickly and that meant being successful in a career."

She had come to the right place. After working briefly as an artist trainee for a silkscreen business and then doing several free-lance jobs for advertising agencies in the San Francisco area, Stenzel landed a job in the graphic design department of Tandem. "I had never seen myself working for a corporation, but Tandem was different. It was only a few years old at the time and there was this incredible high energy, this feeling that anything was possible. It reflected many of the things I had always felt about my own life—that if you worked hard enough at something you could achieve anything."

As Stenzel quickly found, Tandem was fertile territory for such raw ambition. One of her first projects was the design of a company flowchart that laid out Treybig's philosophy for making Tandem a successful corporation, including how to make employees feel part of the organization and how to respect and care for them as individuals. But Stenzel was more than the project's artist. For several weeks, she worked side by side with the company president, "acting as his right arm and giving my input on ideas and philosophies." A bond developed between Stenzel and Treybig, another former Texan who was impressed with his young employee's openness and commitment. Treybig wanted to know what role Stenzel, who was 26 at the time, envisioned for herself in the future. "I told him that someday I wanted to be the art director of a magazine." Treybig didn't see any reason why Stenzel should wait to fulfill her dream. "He wanted to start a new in-house philosophy and strategy magazine for the company and asked me, on the spot, to be the design director. I had only been at the company a year. I thought that maybe he didn't know enough about art and design to realize that I really wasn't experienced enough. But that was true of a lot of people at Tandem who accepted these incredible opportunities even though they were wondering how they would ever do it. You wanted to try anyway. Jim Treybig's enthusiasm made you believe you could do it."

From that moment on, Stenzel's devotion to the community of work became total. Stenzel was managing designers with far more experience than she. In order to keep up she had to work until 9 or 10 p.m. nearly every evening and most weekend days. "My professional experience came a lot differently than I had ever imagined. I had to learn things like production and editing quickly so that I had at least enough knowledge to manage the people working for me." Like many career climbers, Stenzel internalized an image of success that equated efficiency and busyness with achievement. She would quickly learn what she needed to know to get by and then move on to the next project. "I never really got a sense of mastering anything in my field," she admits.

What she had achieved, however, was acceptance into a tight-knit professional culture that seemed, at least for a time, to fulfill most of her needs. Between regular Friday afternoon "beer busts" with colleagues and socializing with a circle of like-minded friends who shared her devotion to a professional cause, Stenzel's life revolved totally around her work community. Even her boyfriend, Bill, now her husband, worked for Tandem as an engineer. For some six years Stenzel's career was so absorbing and exhausting that she didn't feel the desire or inclination to do much else but work. "I was putting far more energy and emotional commitment into my job than even my relationship with Bill. We both worked long hours, and our major bond often seemed to be our devotion to our careers."

The unrelenting pace, fueled, in part, Stenzel now says, by the belief that the "more hours we put in the more successful we were," began to slow down considerably when the magazine came under scrutiny as a likely cost-cutting candidate. "In the early days of the company, it was an important vehicle for expressing an organizational philosophy. But it was no longer vital. I knew that I had to think about moving on to something else." For the first time in her professional life, Stenzel had time on her hands—time to consider where she had been and where she was going. Such crossroads present an ideal opportunity for career climbers to evaluate their next step. Many professionals, however, are so anxious to grab hold of another rung on the success ladder that they fail to use such periods to catch their breath and take stock. Not Stenzel. Despite several opportunities for continued advancement at Tandem, she found herself hesitating to make another leap forward.

During this period Stenzel had begun doing volunteer work for an organization that worked against nuclear weapons proliferation. Although her involvement had come on a whim, the work and surrounding issues were affecting her more deeply than she had imagined. Stenzel had grown up in an environment that emphasized community involvement. Her parents were active in the civil rights movement of the 1950s and 1960s and were part of a group that had brought suit against the local school board in Georgetown, Texas, to force integration. In her pursuit of "a meaningful life," Stenzel now realized, she had pushed aside many of the lessons she had learned from her parents about being part of a larger community. In the community of work she had thrived on for the past six years, there never even seemed to be a reason to turn on the nightly news or read the local newspaper, let alone devote herself to a cause. "I began to see that there was this part of myself I had completely ignored because it didn't fit into this image I had of myself as a career person. I had had the satisfaction of being recognized and rewarded for my contributions and moving up quickly. I was making more money than I ever thought I would be at that point in my life, and was beginning to feel I wanted to start giving something back."

Although Tandem's community of work tended to reinforce an attitude of noninvolvement in outside causes, it also encouraged employees to lead full lives by offering personal leaves and other innovative job arrangements. Stenzel believed that truly commiting herself to a cause would require more than volunteering a few evenings a week. "It was obvious to me that if I was really going to get deeply involved in something outside of work, I needed to devote myself to it fully. I knew I couldn't continue to do my one hundred twenty percent job at Tandem." At about that time, Stenzel learned that a staff editor in another department was interested in job sharing. It was a lower position with considerably reduced responsibility and less pay than her current slot. But the job sharing arrangement meant that Stenzel would only have to work three days a week.

Stenzel's inclination to move into a lesser job also reflected a realistic understanding of what it would take to distance herself from a professional world that had been the center of her life for the past six years. As more professionals are finding, working less is not merely a matter of altering one's schedule. The need to put out sudden fires and meet unexpected deadlines is especially difficult for part-timers in management jobs. Returning to a staff position, where there is typically more flexibility to pick and choose projects, is a more realistic option for a growing number of part-time professionals.

Stenzel's decision to backtrack her career shocked her colleagues and put a strain for a time on her marriage as her husband continued to pursue a traditional career track at Tandem. For Stenzel, however, it offered the sense of meaning and balance she now realized she had been searching for all along. "The most rewarding achievements come from feeling you are part of a larger community and that in some way, beyond your individual professional goals, you are really making a difference."

As many professionals find, backtracking is more than a step down the ladder. It ultimately represents a complete revamping of one's vision of success. Images of glamour and an upward fast track ultimately fade into the background, replaced by a new set of less glossy but ultimately more rewarding pictures. These new images include work that is more inherently meaningful, a family life that is complete and satisfying and a connection to the larger community that makes the community of work seem small and limiting. Since the old rules are no longer relevant, the possible paths toward career success open up dramatically. Back-trackers realize it doesn't matter if they move up, down or sideways—as long as the road they are following is true to their personal notion of a successful life. Many assume the role of career shifter periodically, as they come to see the value of occasionally shaking up their professional identities and exploring new areas that are off the beaten track.

5

• •

The Career Shifter

Shifting careers is not the same as changing careers. The following chapter will not tell you how to leave the predictable world of lawyering, doctoring or business managing behind and tap your long-dormant talents as a rock musician, gourmet chef or nuclear physicist. It will not try to convince you that excitement, adventure and glamour are within your grasp if you take the plunge, give up the profession you have excelled in for a decade or two and follow your heart to your "dream" job.

Some people should, of course, change careers. These are professionals who may have taken a wrong turn from the start—whose aptitudes and interests have little to do with the work they do every day. And there are others who are simply ready for a change; they may be bored with their current profession or ready to embark on a completely new adventure.

Far too many professionals, however, look to career changes as a kind of personal salvation. In many instances they may be avoiding reality in much the same way as the super fast-tracker who believes his life is ruined because he chose the wrong phone system or the carefree dropout who opted for the mailroom rather than a junior partnership so that he could eat his Frosted Flakes in peace. Making a radical career change allows disenchanted professionals to feel they are taking charge of their destinies, when all they may really be doing is covering up what is truly making them unhappy.

For the vast majority of professionals, changing careers is not the answer to finding a more balanced and satisfying professional path. Shifting careers, on the other hand, may be. More than semantics is at work here. Career shifters, unlike career changers, still gain satisfaction and enjoyment from their chosen professions but have confined themselves to an unnecessarily narrow course within that profession. The approach they take is more appropriately labeled career shifting because it involves a refocusing rather than a complete redoing of their professional pursuits. Career changing, by contrast, often requires returning to school and then reestablishing a whole new set of professional contacts to open up doors and help gain solid footing in a new profession. Such changes can take years and are often a major shock to the ego and the pocketbook. Achieving a more balanced life on a slower track, career shifters realize, will not come from completely dismantling their careers and starting over from scratch.

The trick for career shifters is to come up with a workable middle ground. Many people find that with a little tinkering they can turn a career that was making them feel unhappy and overly stressed into a far more satisfying occupation that allows them to assert their true selves both on and off the job. The career shifter's adaptability allows him or her to see opportunity where others may see only obstacles to a satisfying personal and professional life. A career-shifting investment broker, for instance, unhappy with the high-pressure world of financial sales, might adapt her career to a new role as a financial planner, where she would have more control over her work and hours. A lawyer who feels his personality is incompatible with the rat race of a corporate firm could go to work as an in-house attorney for a corporation or as a government lawyer. A somewhat more radical approach might be a shift to a job in academia, where real-life experiences can be applied in a classroom setting. And still others may find a more comfortable fit in a nonprofit organization where skilled professionals can use their training to work for a special cause.

Such shifts allow professionals to apply strengths and skills built up over several years in a setting that is more conducive to their needs, on and off the job. The approach can be used effectively throughout one's career, either to downshift during a time when family needs or other personal interests take priority or simply to try out alternative professional settings. Career shifting can be used on virtually any new success track: A purposely plateaued engineer for a large corporation, for instance, may decide to seek new challenges by moving into an academic arena. Self-employers, as you will see in Chapter 6, frequently shift careers in an effort to find a more comfortable professional setting for making it on their own. Urban escapees (Chapter 7) rely on career shifting to establish professional roots in communites where career options may be more limited. In each case, career shifting allows for professional adjustments that are not as disruptive as a complete career change, while leaving the door open to one's previous career path if returning to a faster track is ever desired.

Performing your professional role on a new stage

More professionals are discovering that the typical route to success in their fields is far from the only acceptable or worthwhile one. Even in occupations bound by centuries of tradition, such as law and medicine, more people are bucking the norm and inventing their own personalized career tracks. Their numbers are still small, but growing. The majority of the nation's 655,191 lawyers still work in private practice, according to a 1985 survey by the American Bar Foundation, with 9.7 percent working for businesses and 8 percent employed by federal or local governments. But there are signs of change. The ten U.S. companies with the largest in-house law departments, for instance, expanded their staffs to 2,750 in 1989, a 6 percent increase over 1988.

Similar trends hold true for medicine, as more doctors are opting to sacrifice the high income of a private practice for the regular hours and more flexible work environments offered by clinics and health maintenance organizations (HMOs). According to a study conducted by the American Medical Association, the number of physicians employed by clinics, HMOs or in other salaried set-ups such as university or government positions grew from 23.5 percent in 1984 to 26.1 percent in 1986, the last year for which such figures are available. But once again, this trend seems to be picking up momentum, particularly as female doctors with children look for alternatives to the long hours required in a private practice. The percentage of women physicians employed by private clinics and other organizations grew from 40.8 percent in 1984 to 48.6 percent in 1986. By comparison, the overall number of male and female solo practitioners has been on a steady decline the last few years, from 43.3 percent in 1984 to 38.5 percent in 1988.

This does go against the trend toward self-employment in other fields, where professionals view striking out on their own as a means of gaining more control over their work and hours (see Chapter 6). For physicians, however, the growing demands and economic constraints of private practice, including rising malpractice insurance, mean solo practitioners must often work seven days a week to keep ahead.

Although there is more acceptance of alternative career paths, within many fields there remains a tendency to look down on those who go against what for so many years was considered the natural career progression. For example, doctors moving to clinics must contend with the perception by some in the field that they are a "poor man's or poor woman's way of practicing," one physician told *American Medical News.* [1] And lawyers must learn to ignore a macho work ethic that looks down on anything that is slightly off the traditional partnership track. Consider the experience of one Manhattan attorney who shifted from a big firm to a government job: "One partner actually told me that he thought I was ruining my life. I was made to feel like I was crazy for giving up the status and money of working for a big firm for what they saw as a lowly government position. When you're at a firm the typical thinking is that you are at the top; that anyone who leaves can't cut it."

Such insular attitudes are particularly pervasive in the academic field. When Eleanor Wachs decided to give up the fight for tenure in her area of American folklore and shift to a more stable career as a museum curator, she had to battle the perceptions of her ivory tower colleagues as well as her long-held beliefs about what defined professional success. "There is a feeling in academia that anyone who is not doing academic work doesn't measure up," says Wachs.

For much of her professional life, Wachs had been trying to do just that. With a master's in American studies and a Ph.D. in folklore and American studies, Wachs had won a rare tenure-track spot in folklore at the University of Massachusetts in Boston. In the spirit of the tenure race she proceeded for the next seven years to immerse herself in an all-consuming academic community of work. She typically worked 15 to 17 hours a day, preparing lectures, writing a book and researching articles. She was driven, like many baby boomers, by an especially strong desire to create her own identity and distance herself from her traditional Brooklyn upbringing, which had done little to encourage professional success for women. Instead, Wachs eagerly made her work her life. With minimal on-the-job structure and no one to tell her when to take a break, she would ignore the alarm clock as it buzzed beside her typewriter and work late into the evening. "I was completely obsessed and absorbed by my work. I hardly had any social life. I barely had a life," says Wachs, who is single.

When the conservative university faculty failed to give Wachs tenure, after deciding that folklore was, in her words, "a luxury subject," Wachs didn't stop pushing. To the contrary—she chose to appeal the case. But the stress of going through the tenure process, spending long nights working on her book and now attempting to appeal the decision not to give her tenure all came crashing down on Wachs one evening when she was rushed to the hospital in an ambulance. "I was hyperventilating and having serious headaches. I was just emotionally and physically exhausted," she recalls. "When I was sitting in the hospital being put through tests, it finally hit me. I kept asking myself, 'What am I doing here?' "

In highly specialized fields like folklore, it isn't uncommon for people not to get tenure. "I've had friends who didn't get it and just moved on to another university and started at the bottom again on $18,000 a year. Even though I love my field, I knew that taking that route would not be healthy for me."

For Wachs, though, there was never any thought of giving up the field of folklore entirely. As a child she spent weekends and afternoons wandering through the exhibits of local museums, reading folktales and studying the customs of different cultures. For the past few years, Wachs had been doing consulting work on the side for several local museums and found it interesting, stimulating and remarkably sane work. Career shifters typically keep their options open by regularly gaining experience and maintaining contacts in areas outside of their immediate job. As a result, when it comes time to make a shift, the transition is likely to be smoother than it often is for other downshifters. In Wachs's case, the museum seemed a logical stage on which to transfer her extensive skills in folklore. She easily got a job as curator of exhibits for the Commonwealth Museum in Boston and left the competitive, unstructured world of academia for a nine-to-five position, taking a $6,000 pay cut.

For most people, a primary motivation behind making a career shift is to gain more flexibility over their hours, not less. But Wachs's story shows why it is important not to simply follow the latest trend when making a career shift. As we will see later in the chapter, academia can be an ideal place to shift *into* for those trying to balance work and family responsibilities—for the very reason that it does not confine them to a set schedule. In Wachs's case, however, the structure of her new job, which included having a boss for the first time in many years, while difficult to adjust to at first, helped her break out of her workaholic lifestyle. "For me, at this point, having a nine-to-five job is healthier. When I come home at night, I can leave the work behind and start focusing on developing a social life. I am realizing that there are other sides to me besides my professional identity." Wachs, in fact, has discovered that there is a "whole world out there after work." She goes on dates and out to dinner with friends, she takes adult education classes in areas such as dance and cooking, spends times decorating her condo and occasionally even teaches night school.

Wachs has found that her work can be involving and stimulating without completely dominating her life. Putting together exhibits allows her to combine a variety of skills and interests and have more direct, hands-on involvement than in her former academic role. For an exhibit on black history in Massachusetts, Wachs's job included everything from collecting the documents and artifacts to writing the text for the exhibit to selecting the music and visuals for the film portions of the show. "I'm in heaven doing this stuff. There's nothing I love more than going to places like the Smithsonian and searching for pieces of history, and then putting the whole thing together," she says.

Wachs doesn't like to think that she has given up academia completely, and imagines herself shifting back in some capacity in the future. This zigzag path typifies the career progression of the highly adaptable career shifter. Take the case of John Nelson. Throughout his career as an economist, Nelson has periodically shifted to new professional stages. After graduate school he started out on a traditional path, working as an economist for Republic National Bank in New York, with ambitions of building a career in international economics. But after four years at the bank, Nelson knew that if his career was going to progress, at least according to the traditional mindset, he would have to switch from economics to the higher stakes area of pure banking. Although the financial payoffs were enticing, even then, while still in his 20s, Nelson was wary of getting trapped on a career track that would require more travel and longer hours the higher up he moved. "To advance in the bank I would have had to get into some form of trading or lending that would have involved more commitment of time and increased travel overseas. I had met a woman, my wife now, who wasn't interested in that kind of lifestyle, and I was beginning to think I wasn't either. Although the money would have been great, I could see already that it wasn't worth getting home at nine or ten every night, working weekends and traveling all the time. I wanted more of a life."

His solution was to find a completely different stage for his financial skills. He combined his love of numbers with his curiosity about politics and went to work as a financial adviser to Carol Bellamy, then Manhattan city councilwoman and a former mayoral candidate. Most of us worry that interrupting the traditional professional path, as Nelson did, would cut off our options and close off our prospects for future success. Instead, we tell ourselves that we will have time to "play a part" once we have proven our professional worth—only to discover that the higher we climb, the tougher it becomes to break away. Nelson, on the other hand, felt it was the ideal time in his young career to take a risk. He and his wife, Janet, a free-lance photographer, were both highly devoted to their work and saw the next few years before they had children as a perfect time to try out different areas of interest and work long hours if that was what was required. Neither, at that point, was in particular need of a downshift.

In fact, working for Bellamy was far more hectic than Nelson's job at the bank, especially during periods of budget negotiations when he would often stay at the office through the night. The difference was that he never viewed his job with Bellamy as a long-term career, but as an interesting professional interlude that he could pour himself into for a few years. "I had always wanted to learn about politics and I was young enough to try something different for a few years. It was more publicly spirited and exciting than what I was doing at the bank," recalls Nelson, who is now in his mid-30s.

Several months before his wife gave birth to their son, Nelson began thinking that perhaps it was time to make another career shift. Janet planned to cut back her successful photography career to four days a week and both agreed that Nelson would also have to find a more flexible work environment that would leave him more time to help care for their new baby. Again, the idea was to take advantage of the skills he had developed working at the bank and for Bellamy, and transfer them to a setting where he would have more control over his hours. He took a job as an economic analyst with the Port Authority of New York and New Jersey, a position that appealed to him for several reasons. First, he knew that public-sector jobs typically offered a more generous work environment than the private sector when it came to issues like childcare. Nelson also knew that the research position, as opposed to one in management, would give him the flexibility he needed to get his job done in the context of what was now a more demanding personal life. "The hours of most research jobs are fairly predictable, since you are rarely called to an unexpected meeting or have an unexpected deadline come up," says Nelson.

When he interviewed for the position, Nelson was upfront about what he was looking for. "I directly asked them what kind of hours were typical and was told that the ethic of the place was that people work long hours or overtime totally on a discretionary basis. It is up to each individual." In fact, shortly after Nelson started his job at the Port Authority, he bought his own personal computer and began working at home whenever possible. "I discovered that my superiors were flexible enough so that if I wanted to do research at home in the evenings after my son was in bed and come in a little later in the mornings on an ad hoc basis, they were willing to accommodate that." Because the hours of his job were predictable, Nelson didn't get himself trapped by the kind of so-called flexible schedule that allows professionals to merely shift the stresses to different parts of the day.

Nelson also thinks he will some day return to the private sector or possibly politics when his two children are older and his priorities shift yet again. Rather than closing off his options, career shifting has broadened Nelson's experience, increased his professional marketability and given him greater control over his life beyond work.

When the classroom calls

One of the primary goals of career shifting is to gain more flexibility over one's hours on the job—although, as we saw with Wachs, that is not always the case. For most career climbers, however, searching for a balanced integration between personal and work life and more freedom to learn and explore within their fields, flexibility is crucial.

During the next decade, professionals searching for control and flexibility will find an abundance of opportunities in academia, which is facing growing faculty shortages. An estimated 330,000 new faculty members are expected to be hired by university and college campuses across the country by the year 2004 as two major trends converge: retirement of the massive numbers of professors who were hired during the 1950s and 1960s and expansion of the student base as both older students pursuing second careers and the kids of baby boomers head for college. The University of California system, for instance, plans to add three new campuses in the next 15 years, and the California State University system will add nine. The increasing need for faculty also means that salaries will be on the rise. Assistant professors saw their salaries increase 7.8 percent in the 1989–90 academic year to an average of $32,960; full-professor pay went up 6.9 percent to $53,540.

All of this spells tremendous opportunity for professionals seeking new challenges and a more flexible setting for their career pursuits. Jordan Kurland, associate general secretary of the American Association of University Professors, says the environment is comparable to that of 25 years ago when "academe was growing like mad." It was not uncommon during that period, says Kurland, for a retired military officer with a background in electrical engineering to be brought on at the university level as a math instructor. Today, similar opportunities await corporate executives, senior attorneys and seasoned journalists who wish to transfer their skills to the classroom. Kurland says salaries will typically be higher for such professionals by an average of about $5,000 compared to other nontenured instructors without "real life" experience, but could be much more than that for those with a well-known name or proven expertise in a given field.

Still, one of the biggest obstacles for most professionals shifting into academia will be the all but certain drop in salary. When Kathleen Goeppinger gave up her position as vice-president of human resource operations for the Chicago retailer Carson Pirie Scott & Company, at age 38, to assume a full-time faculty position at Loyola University in Chicago, her salary dropped to one-quarter of her corporate paycheck. But the flexibility of her teaching schedule has allowed Goeppinger to supplement her income with outside consulting projects—especially during the summer months. "I took a huge cut to come to the university, but over time, with consulting, speeches and some publishing my income is fairly close to what it was in corporate life. You just get it in different ways." Like many downshifters, Goeppinger and her husband, John, a human resources consultant, have not so much downscaled their lifestyles as plateaued them. "It's just little things, like my husband deciding to keep the car an extra year. But it wasn't a big deal. We probably should have done it anyway."

What has changed dramatically since Goeppinger made the shift to academia is the quality of her life. "Just being able to take the morning off if I want to and spend time in the park with my kids, even if it means working later in the evening, has made an enormous difference in the overall sanity of my life," says Goeppinger, who had been almost completely absorbed by the community of work during her nearly 20 years with Carson Pirie Scott. "Both my husband and I had developed this pattern for ourselves where we didn't seem to need much else. We would leave early for work in the morning and come home late. Our outside involvements were minimal, but we loved our work and felt happy with our lives."

Even after the couple had their first child, when Goeppinger was in her late 30s, not much changed—at least initially. Goeppinger went back to work almost immediately and resumed her old routine, with the added pressure of having a child to care for. Her new and conflicting needs started to take a toll, however. To her surprise, she found herself feeling increasingly dissatisfied. "I remember one day dropping my daughter off with the childcare person at six in the morning because I had a seven o'clock breakfast meeting and then not getting home until nine at night because I also had a meeting that evening. I was missing her a lot, but when I would get to work I would just push those feelings out of my mind. I had a job to do, people were making demands of me and I was running from meeting to meeting, so I didn't have time to dwell on it. But it was always painful every time I dropped her off in the morning at the crack of dawn. It was always in the back of my mind."

Goeppinger realized she had to find a way to cut back. She knew that her high position and ego involvement in her career would have made it extremely difficult, both practically and emotionally, to backtrack within her company. "I knew the corporate culture wouldn't have tolerated someone like me stepping back, and it wasn't in my nature either." Goeppinger interviewed with a few other corporations but quickly decided that it would be "more of the same." During this period, she also sought out the advice of friends and mentors. One of them was her former faculty adviser at Loyola, where she had received her master's degree and doctorate. He suggested that she ease into her decision by doing some part-time teaching in the university's industrial relations department to see if she would feel comfortable outside of a corporate setting.

Goeppinger thrived in her new role. "I discovered that there were a million transferable skills coming from the corporate world. I believe I am a better teacher because my experience is such that, while it isn't textbook, it is real management." Testing her skills part-time for a full year gave Goeppinger the confidence to leave the company that had employed her for nearly 20 years and go to work as a full-time assistant professor in industrial relations for Loyola.

For Goeppinger and her husband, who left his corporate job soon afterwards to work full-time as a consultant from the couple's suburban Chicago home, taking that year to decide also gave them time to work out their finances. The Goeppingers determined that the nest egg they had built up during their years on the corporate fast track gave them an adequate cushion to absorb the large income drop—whether or not Kathleen maintained her outside consulting work. Like the Goeppingers, many career shifters find that preparing themselves ahead of time, if possible, can help ease the inevitable financial adjustments.

In the months before Brad Lewis decided to shift from his high-paying job as an attorney for a top Los Angeles firm to a position with the U.S. Attorney's office in Sacramento, he and his wife, Victoria, also a lawyer, consciously began altering their lifestyles. Says Lewis: "I knew I would be taking a 40 percent pay cut, so we just figured out how much we would be taking home and shoved the rest into a savings account. We had to adjust our thinking both practically and emotionally. When you make a lot of money and get used to a particular way of living, it is difficult to just pull back cold turkey."

On the other hand, for those seeking a lifestyle change as well as a professional shift, academia is also an ideal vehicle for maintaining a career outside of expensive and stressful urban areas. (This approach will be examined in more depth in Chapter 7, The Urban Escapee.) In his new job as head of the media center at DePauw University in Greencastle, Indiana, Ken Bode, for instance, now makes about one-quarter of the $200,000 annual income he could have expected if he had stayed on as national political correspondent for NBC News. But he says his family has barely felt the income difference because the cost of living in Greencastle is so much lower than it had been in Washington, D.C. Bode and his wife, Margo, a writer, bought their four-bedroom home on a tree-lined Greencastle street, ten minutes' drive from the DePauw University campus, for under $100,000. The same house might have cost three or four times that in the Washington area. "The entire family of four can eat for a week for a total of forty-five dollars. We don't go out to restaurants anymore where you have to drop sixty dollars for four people. Now if we drop twenty-five dollars when we go out, we've had a really good time. It is just an easier lifestyle."

For both Bode and Goeppinger, the toughest part of shifting to academia wasn't the drop in income but the drop in professional stature. It was the little things that bothered Goeppinger at first—like the size of her new office. "I went from a wonderful, big office to a very small one. I remember just sitting there during the first few months and saying to myself, 'What did you do this to yourself for?' " And after years of making her way to the top of the corporate world and establishing a strong professional identity, Goeppinger suddenly found herself back at the bottom of another career totem pole, wondering if she would someday get tenure. Her response, for a while, was to cling to her old identity. It took Goeppinger an entire year before she stopped introducing herself as "an instructor at Loyola and the former corporate vice-president of human resources for Carson Pirie Scott." The response of others in her field didn't help. "I remember entering this huge auditorium of five hundred people to give a talk and being introduced as the 'former . . . ' "

Bode too had to suffer through the predictable bafflement of colleagues and friends who couldn't understand why he had left a "dream job" for a position at a small midwestern university. "Inevitably people say things like 'He's burned out' or 'He couldn't cut it.' But the truth is, when I look at the people who are doing the talking, they are the ones who have given over virtually their entire beings for their jobs. They are the ones who haven't had a Thanksgiving dinner home in years; who are single because they can't sustain a relationship because their jobs always come first." In one sense, Bode was as committed as any of those colleagues to his work. He loved his job at NBC—so much so that he found it increasingly difficult to make time for much else.

During his career at the network, Bode became known for his "out-in-the-field" spots. Rather than covering politics from Washington, he went out to the towns and cities across America to report on the real issues facing real people. It was exciting and compelling work. But it required Bode to be on the road at least once a week. "The hard part," he says, "was checking with my kids each night to find out whether they studied for their spelling tests." Bode had always prided himself on being an involved father in a field where few people had healthy family lives. But as Bode's success grew and he was in greater demand, it became harder and harder to set limits and spend the kind of time he wanted to with his wife and two young daughters.

His misgivings had actually been building for several years. "There were a lot of strings gathering in my mind—lots of little things telling me that maybe I should be doing something different," recalls Bode. There was the time his daughter Josie, then 3, crawled into the suitcase Bode had sprawled across the bed as he was packing for another trip. "She said to me, 'Dad, don't take any more dumb trips. Tell your dumb bosses at NBC that you can't travel anymore.' It broke my heart." Then there was the day Bode arrived for a morning interview at a downtown Washington hotel, only to be confronted with an interview subject who "looked completely hung over, like he'd knocked down a fifth of scotch. I said, 'What in the hell happened to you?' He said, 'Yesterday, I drove my daughter to college and when I came home I went into her room and cried. I just knew right then that with all the successes and busy times I had, it was over, my possibilities of really knowing that kid were over.' "

But it was one incident, more than any of the others, that solidified Bode's decision to make a shift. It was during the 1988 presidential primaries and Bode was in Boston for a debate after covering the California races. Throughout the primary season, from September to June, he had maintained a hectic travel schedule. On this particular trip Bode had already been away from home for three weeks and had told his superiors at the network that he needed a break. He was promised the following weekend off. When he spoke to his then 10-year-old daughter Matilda that evening he assured her that he would be home the next night for her Glee Club performance. "I said, 'Yes, absolutely. NBC promised me and I promise you.' " But just as he hung up, the phone rang. It was NBC. "They had a story they wanted me to do for the nightly news on Friday. I asked them if they could get someone else to do it, like Chris Wallace or Lisa Meyers, and pointed out that they had promised me the following few days off. But they really twisted my arm and insisted that I had to do it because I was the national political correspondent."

Bode did the story and missed his daughter's Glee Club performance. The next morning he called a friend who counseled people considering career changes. "I loved my work, but I just knew that one day I was going to come home and my oldest daughter would be packing for college."

He began to consider various options. One was to stay in

Washington doing occasional special reports and free-lancing. But the pressures of trying to cut back in a town like Washington where he would be surrounded daily by high-profile colleagues did not appeal to him. "Washington is a city that requires you to live at a certain pace and maintain a certain income. With everyone else around me moving at that pace it would have been very difficult to just pull back." When a friend informed him that De-Pauw was looking for someone to head its new center for contemporary media it seemed like the perfect opportunity for Bode, who grew up in Iowa and missed the camaraderie and sense of community found in a smalltown setting. "My family was skeptical, but they were willing to give it a try. Now they couldn't be happier. The girls both play on their school basketball teams, Matilda's also on the volleyball team and played Dorothy in her school's production of *The Wizard of Oz.* No one wants to go back."

For Bode, like Goeppinger, shifting to academia allowed him to leave behind the pressures to succeed along a narrowly defined career path, without having to start completely from scratch. Furthermore, the flexibility provided by a university setting has given both Bode and Goeppinger the opportunity to reinvent success in a way that better meets their personal and professional needs.

Goeppinger overcame her initial "identity crisis" by learning to focus on the new rewards of an academic career and a fuller outside life. The respect and support she receives from students has gone a long way toward replacing the perks of a corporate career. "The students look up to me because I've been there and can really teach them something. The reinforcement I get from them is more than enough to keep me committed to this." Goeppinger also feels that she has a perspective on the tenure race that would have been difficult if she hadn't already proven herself professionally. "I want very much to get tenure, but it isn't an all-consuming thing for me." Today, she has time for interests beyond work and family that help her maintain that perspective. She serves on the boards of such organizations as the Boys and Girls Clubs of Chicago and several professional associations, as well as doing other volunteer work.

Bode has found that having greater control of his schedule has not only given him more time to spend with his family but has allowed him to keep a foot in the profession he loves. "The university has encouraged me to stay involved as an active journalist and use my voice to comment on issues in the media, to continue to write or do television in a way that the students might be involved and benefit from my experience." He has written op-ed pieces on various political issues for the *New York Times* and other publications and has signed on with CNN to do monthly features on the Bush administration—with a middle America perspective. "I'm finding that there are ways to stay involved without having to kill myself on the network's schedule."

Today, when Bode thinks about those former colleagues who were dismayed by his departure, an image comes to mind that automatically reinforces his decision. It is an image of a bleary-eyed network correspondent answering the phone by his bed at 4:30 a.m. In minutes, the correspondent is on his feet, grabbing a make-up case and heading for the studio. Two hours later he is on the air for the "Today" show with a microphone tucked behind his ear and his mind temporarily cleared after too many steamy gulps of coffee. It is an image of success that defines the life of a network correspondent—the television version of the "gotta run, I'll call you, we'll do lunch" persona of the eighties professional. But for Bode it represents the most empty kind of success. "I was a success," he says, "by every measure except those by which every human being should measure his real successes—that is, the joy of your family life and the pleasure of living life completely."

Turning a cause into a career

Career shifters achieve balance by not allowing themselves to be controlled by one career track, with one set of goals and one notion of achievement. Instead, they use their professional skills as leverage for exploring new aspects of their fields and tapping into different—and perhaps more worthwhile—areas of interest. Many are finding a particularly satisfying fit in the nonprofit sector, where professionals with management expertise can move quickly into vital and challenging roles.

One important aspect of reinventing success is working toward goals that are inherently more meaningful. Despite their outward successes, many career climbers complain of feeling detached from the actual work they are doing. "I am constantly rewarded for my work, but there is no real sense that what I am doing actually means anything. Sometimes I think that it is completely irrelevant even to my employer," says one New York marketing executive. Such sentiments are leading more and more corporate players away from the private sector and into jobs they feel personally committed to.

During the last two decades, nonprofits grew faster than either private business or government, employing a total of 7.2 million people in 1986, or approximately 1 in 16 working Americans, according to the Independent Sector, a Washington, D.C., research organization. A 1987 Labor Department study projected that the nonprofit labor force would reach 9.3 million in 1995. Beyond the sheer numbers, however, something else is happening in the nonprofit world that is making it an increasingly enticing place for anyone with a business background. As competition for money intensifies, these organizations are professionalizing their efforts. As a result, people with skills in financial planning, marketing and management are in demand and can draw increasingly high salaries.

Nonprofits technically include major health and educational institutions such as hospitals and private schools. But the greatest changes have taken place among the less visible community groups and special-interest associations. Salaries have risen dramatically in the last decade as even small organizations bid for people with business skills. An executive director of a consumer advocacy group with as few as ten employees, such as a state organization that lobbies for stricter drunk-driving laws, earned an average of $46,500 in the late 1980s, according to a recent survey sponsored by the Society of Nonprofit Organizations in Madison, Wisconsin. The highest salaries can generally be found in urban areas where competition for top talent is stiffest. A 1988 survey of Washington, D.C., nonprofit organizations by the consulting firm Cordom Associates found that executive directors earned an average of $112,501, compared with $81,843 in 1982, the first year for which figures were available.

Still, while salaries are improving, in most cases the initial shift to a nonprofit organization is likely to result in a significant income change. Bill Misenhimer saw his $55,000 salary drop by $21,000 when he left his position as manager in Xerox's Los Angeles-based printing business division in 1984 to work full-time for AIDS Project L.A. (APLA). Since that time, however, Misenhimer's income has climbed past where it had been at Xerox.

But money was the least of Misenhimer's concerns when he took a leave from his job at Xerox, where, at the age of 32, he was the youngest employee on the management payroll in his division, and decided to devote his life to fighting AIDS. "I remember sitting in a meeting one day and saying to myself, 'What am

I doing worrying about how to get copiers out to people when I have friends who are dying?' "

Until that moment, Bill Misenhimer's life had progressed pretty much according to plan. With a degree in accounting, he had spent more than a decade in finance administration at such companies as Pacific Telephone, BMW and Xerox. His career was unquestionably the center of his life. "I took a lot of pride in my work and was a workaholic. I worked all the time." Misenhimer believes he would have continued indefinitely along that path if it hadn't been for an incident that brought the AIDS problem a little too close to home. His own fear of the disease was first tested in 1982, when Misenhimer, who is gay, developed a flu that he couldn't shake. Terrified that this could be that horrible illness that was just gaining attention in the press, he went to a doctor and was told he had a virus associated with the "gay-related disease." Although further tests revealed that it was nothing of the sort and that Misenhimer was fine, his initial scare and the ignorance his experience revealed about the disease spurred the once strait-laced business executive to get involved.

While still working at Xerox, Misenhimer organized a letter-writing campaign to federal, state and local officials, and led a petition drive at the Los Angeles gay pride parade that drew more than 14,000 signatures. Between doing volunteer work for AIDS organizations and watching friends grow ill and die from the disease, Misenhimer found it increasingly difficult to focus on his job. He applied for and was awarded a nine-month social service leave, as part of a program offered by Xerox, and eventually resigned completely from the company to devote himself full-time to AIDS Project L.A. Such leave programs, while still rare at most companies, are gaining popularity particularly in the competitive high-tech fields. IBM, Tandem and several other firms offer a variety of personal leave options that provide an excellent opportunity for career shifters to explore related areas before deciding on a permanent move.

Misenhimer's experience over the next few years points out both the potential pitfalls and extremely positive rewards of turning a cause into a career. As Misenhimer found, professionals who take such paths must continally work to set limits. Those who successfully pull it off find they can translate valuable skills gained in the private sector into an area that is inherently more in line with their personal interests and values. When Misenhimer first joined APLA, it was a new organization in need of direction and professionalism. Misenhimer's traditional corporate background—by the time he left Xerox he was overseeing a staff of 26—combined with his enthusiasm for the cause, was exactly what the group was looking for. His managerial skills proved invaluable at APLA, where Misenhimer used his leadership abilities and political savvy to win the favor of APLA's board and the gay community, and to get a series of impressive projects off the ground.

Misenhimer had gone to APLA to handle finance administration—a highly focused job that he believed would allow him to keep his workaholic tendencies in check. But within a month of his arrival, the organization's executive director left and Misenhimer was put in charge. His life from then on became completely consumed by the AIDS crisis. "At the end of two years, I was at the point of burnout. It had gotten to me in the worst way. Seeing people die all the time at a young age and working the crazy hours I did were just too much. My emotions started to interfere with my ability to work with people. I was angry all the time, and seeing more and more people die every day just made me angrier."

As Misenhimer found while at APLA and John Nelson discovered during his stint with Carol Bellamy, there are times when putting career first makes sense. Working to fight AIDS, after all, was not the kind of job Misenhimer would ever be able to completely leave at the office, especially since it was so closely associated with his own life. At the same time, he knew he had to figure out a way not to let the job overtake him.

After two years of "eating, sleeping and breathing" APLA, Misenhimer decided to shift to a position as executive director of a smaller and lower-key organization, the American Foundation for AIDS Research (AMFAR). Despite the resentment such moves can cause, Misenhimer has found the only way to maintain his own health while working on an emotionally draining cause is to occasionally insist on pulling back.

In fact, Misenhimer has made a practice of regularly shifting in and out of positions when he sensed he was burning out or wanted to start emphasizing areas outside of work more. When his closest friend of 20 years was diagnosed with AIDS and died within a year, Misenhimer did what he felt was best for his own health and sanity—he took a nine-month leave to travel and clear his mind, subsidizing himself with consulting work for both AIDS organizations. "No matter how much you want to contribute, there comes a point where you have to make a choice about what's good for you as a person. When I left AMFAR to go on leave a lot of people felt I was deserting them, and there continued to be a fair amount of resentment when I came back."

Upon his return, Misenhimer knew that if he was going to continue to make AIDS his career, it would have to be in a highly contained job that did not threaten to throw his emotions into turmoil on nearly a daily basis. Considering his workaholic tendencies, Misenhimer, like Eleanor Wachs, felt the best course was to shift into a job that came with its own clear boundaries and limits. The slot he had initially been hired to fill at APLA—chief financial officer—was open again. It seemed to offer the perfect solution. The position was not nearly as visible as his former post heading the organization, but Misenhimer didn't mind being out of the limelight. "Right now my job just involves making sure people raise the right amount of money and use it wisely. It is an important position, where I can really be a help to the organization. But it doesn't invade every second of my life."

Because of the humanistic orientation of nonprofit organizations, most are better able to accommodate personal needs than private firms. The type of shifting that Misenhimer orchestrated between the two AIDS groups would have been far more difficult in a bottom-line, more rigidly structured corporate hierarchy. The case of one California woman further demonstrates this point. Having worked in marketing and retailing for several years, she had been searching for a part-time position in her field when she decided to turn to the nonprofit sector. Within days she found a job with a small advocacy group for the homeless, which was looking for someone to open and manage a used clothing store full-time. With a little finagling, she was able to come up with an acceptable solution: Volunteers from a nearby college, eager for the experience, would work the hours she didn't want. The organization agreed to turn the job into a part-time position for her.

Career shifters, no matter what route they take, achieve control over their work environment by learning to be adaptable. While they may have a broad set of professional goals, they are willing to let those goals bend and give a little as their lives move in new and perhaps unexpected directions. At some point they may decide that the best way to achieve control and balance is to strike out on their own. Gaining more control through self-employment, however, may mean making tradeoffs in other areas.

6

• •

The Self-Employer

Our images of success during the 1980s were heavily influenced by the hard-driving, win-at-all-costs young entrepreneur. As we have seen, professionals like Matthew Simon, the whiz kid who built his own million-dollar real-estate business by the time he was 24, and all those other under-30 tycoons who populated the high-tech and retail industries during the past decade, created a standard for professional success that seemed hard to match. These young fast-trackers, racing through their 20s on four hours of sleep a night, were the last people to think about balancing their lives or downshifting their careers. For them, work was the center of everything, and growth was the only acceptable measure of success.

In recent years, however, entrepreneurship in this country has undergone an evolution. The swashbuckling business daredevil who worked grueling hours and risked all for the power and glory of controlling his own fate—and whose superhuman efforts often left him burnt out or bankrupt—has been overshadowed by the lower-key self-employer who approaches entrepreneurship primarily as a lifestyle decision. "There has unquestionably been a huge shift in the number of people turning to self-employment as a more reasonable way to conduct their careers and live their lives," says James Cabera, president of the executive outplacement firm Drake Beam Morin.

These entrepreneurs are less inclined to pursue aggressive business growth. In some cases they may even avoid it, not wanting to get bogged down in administrative headaches that would force them to borrow more money and hire more employees. Instead, they are content to expand their businesses just enough to make a reasonable living while maintaining a manageable schedule. Such professionals are rarely motivated by money or even the fantasy of fulfilling an entrepreneurial dream. Instead, they view self-employment as a workable vehicle for achieving the control and flexibility that eluded them on the corporate career track. This version of the entrepreneurial dream, writes Rosabeth Moss Kanter in *When Giants Learn to Dance,* revolves around "autonomy rather than wealth, around 'being my own boss' rather than building an empire."[1]

Despite the eighties stereotype of the money-driven, power-hungry entrepreneur, recent studies have shown that the majority of people starting businesses today are motivated by something quite different. In a survey of some 3,000 new business owners by the National Federation of Independent Businesses, 54 percent said that having "greater control over their life" was among the most important reasons for choosing entrepreneurship and 32 percent said being able to "live where and how I like" was at the top of their list. By contrast, only 19 percent said earning a lot of money and gaining more respect and recognition were primary motivators.

A variety of economic and social changes during the past decade have enabled professional men and women to approach self-employment as a relatively risk-free alternative to a corporate career. The growth of the service economy—expected to account for 80 percent of all jobs in this country by the year 2000, according to the Bureau of Labor Statistics—has created entrepreneurial opportunities for just about anyone who can afford a personal computer, a telephone and a fax machine. The response has been staggering: From 1980 to 1987, according to the BLS, the total number of nonfarm self-employed workers jumped nearly 20 percent from 6.8 million to 8.2 million. Women entrepreneurs accounted for by far the most significant growth, with a 35.5 percent increase since 1980 compared with a 13 percent increase in the number of self-employed men.

For both men and women, self-employment offers a workable alternative to an increasingly unstable corporate environment. "When you continually feel in danger of losing your job because of organizational reshufflings and mergers, the relative risks of self-employment are minimized," says Frank Swain, former chief counsel for advocacy of the Small Business Administration. More than anything else, self-employment allows professionals to create a world that accommodates their needs, in a way that a corporation almost never can. This is particularly true for women, whose employers generally remain ill-equipped and ill-prepared to help them deal with the realities of combining motherhood and career. Self-employment provides a convenient and acceptable escape hatch for women and men who wish to ease back professionally while their children are young.

In recent years, women professionals have been especially drawn to the flexibility and professional challenges offered by self-employment. Today, in fact, one out of three sole proprietorships is owned by women. Rather than struggling to achieve a balanced life in male-dominated corporations, these women are discovering they can create their own communities of work where integration of professional and personal needs is considered essential. In many cases, that means locating their businesses closer to home to allow for a more natural flow between work and family. According to *Working Woman* magazine, these women are bringing "big-city sophistication to suburban towns by creating stores that feature innovative displays and selective merchandise. They choose a business that will challenge their creative energy and provide the products and services lacking in their community—often ones they have wished for personally. And in so doing they relieve the stressful 'superwoman' syndrome by being closer to their children and feeling more in charge of their own time." [2]

Running their own show also gives women the opportunity to circumvent that much-maligned macho work ethic and build organizations that are more humanistic and less hierarchical. When Rita Irons, former corporate vice-president of human resources for the publishing firm John Wiley & Sons, decided to form her own consulting group with another woman, the goal was to "create a collaborative and open environment with no real hierarchy." Today, her New York-based Align Inc. employs about seven women, most of whom work part-time on such projects as helping client companies relocate and set up new human resource programs. All employees of the firm are essentially partners who get a share of firm profits at the end of each year. "We want to create very flexible opportunities for women at different stages of their lives. Two of the women here recently had babies and work part-time. In my case, work right now is a primary focus because my children are grown and I don't have a lot of outside obligations. We want to show that women can have other options besides dropping out or getting on some mommy track. They can still be very involved in their jobs and grow in their work without putting in fifty or sixty hours a week."

In contrast to the balance sought by the back-tracker, the stability and continuity cherished by the plateauer and the adaptability perfected by the career shifter, the self-employer believes that true happiness and genuine success are achieved only when one has the autonomy to set his or her own course—and then, on a whim, to change directions. Because of their independent natures, these professionals are often attracted to the free-agent lifestyle of the self-employed. But as downshifters, their desire to gain more control over their careers and freedom in other areas of their lives leads them to search out new and creative methods of achieving that independence.

Men and women who choose to downshift through self-employment see it as an ideal way to keep growing both personally and professionally. But that does not mean setting themselves on a high-risk course that may or may not net them the biggest financial return in the shortest period of time. Instead, their goal is to do what it takes to build a successful business, while eliminating many of the pressures of starting from scratch. Many are responding by coming up with new twists on the traditional entrepreneurial theme. Their goal is to cut out or at least curtail the most stressful aspect of self-employment—selling yourself to bring in new business. They may, for instance, subcontract out to a few steady clients or hook up with a temporary employment agency that specializes in finding work for professionals. Such options provide the freedom of self-employment without forcing them to assume yet another all-consuming professional role.

Creating your own role

Across from Robin Schirmer's desk, propped up carefully on a windowsill cluttered with stacks of legal documents, is an icon to another age: a faded board game with pink lettering. "What shall I be?" it asks. "The Exciting Game of Career Girls." Schirmer opens the cardboard game box and pulls out a pile of heart-shaped cards intended to provide career guidance to young girls, circa 1966. The options inside turn out to be rather limited: teacher, model, actress, airline hostess, nurse, ballet dancer. If you are emotional, says one card, you'll make a good actress or model. If you are a hard worker, reads another, you are destined to be a ballet dancer or a nurse. And if you are neat, you'll have an exciting future as an airline hostess, teacher, nurse or model.

"It was a gag gift from a friend," explains Schirmer. "It's a good conversation piece." But Schirmer is the first to recognize its potent irony. For much of her life, she blindly acted out whatever role was handed her—until deciding a few years ago to create her own.

Like many women today in their 30s and 40s, Schirmer, now in her late 30s, has felt the constant tug of opposing expectations. From her tradition-minded parents came the message that she should go to college to "meet a nice boy," settle down and have a family. When she attended Valparaiso University in Indiana, Schirmer never had a set career in mind. She majored in art and, true to her parents' wishes, met and, at age 22, married John Benous, a legal-aid lawyer. But Schirmer, who even then, in a small act of rebellion, kept her own name, started to feel restless. She sensed the pull of a society that now said women her age should have clear career goals. What she knew about law from her husband and his friends intrigued her, so she decided to enroll in Chicago Kent Law School. She ended up graduating second in her class.

From then on, Schirmer became immersed in a new, although in some ways equally restrictive set of expectations—those imposed by the fast track. "Because I did so well in law school, all these doors flew open for me. I could have gotten a job at just about any firm in the city," says Schirmer. She accepted a position with the medium-sized Chicago law firm of

Sachnoff, Weaver & Rubenstein (now Sachnoff & Weaver), where she spent six years as a high-paid associate handling multi-million-dollar real-estate deals.

Schirmer dutifully played by the rules of the game and progressed quickly and impressively in her career. "I was always trying to play the good girl," she says. She took a brief respite after her son was born—a two-month maternity leave plus four and a half months on a part-time schedule—but quickly returned to the round-the-clock grind of the billings race. "When I look back on it now, the life I was leading was pretty sick. I would actually be happy and smiling at the end of a fifteen-hour day because I would get to bill so much time." But it wasn't until the word went out that Schirmer would soon be tapped for partner that she started to take a hard look at the life she was leading. "The idea of becoming a partner really didn't even excite me. I knew something was wrong."

As we have seen, such career opportunities often trigger professionals to start taking stock. Back-tracker Wendy Osborn Stenzel, for example, decided to switch from a management position to a part-time staff job when she was faced with the possibility of promotion at Tandem Computer. Especially for professionals like Stenzel and Schirmer, whose success was quick and unexpected, it is often necessary to pull back in order to get their lives on a track they feel comfortable with. What mattered most for Schirmer, however, was not only cutting down her work load but being able to call her own shots and do work she "felt good about." "I was tired of always living my life according to someone else's plan for me. First, it was my parents. Then, it was by the rules of a supposedly successful legal career." Schirmer began to realize that she had unshackled herself from the trap of a traditional upbringing only to fall into a new career trap. She began searching for a way out.

During that same period, Valerie Fisher, a colleague of

Schirmer's, had begun to feel equally at odds with her life. She had maintained her practice while raising three young children and for the last few years had attempted the precarious balancing act of part-time work. Fisher was beginning to feel that her naturally driven, perfectionist personality was not conducive to setting the kind of limits necessary to make a part-time position work. "I always felt guilty when I was at home that I wasn't putting in as many hours as I could have been in the office and when I was in the office I felt guilty that I wasn't putting in as many hours as I should be at home," says Fisher, who is in her early 40s. "In some ways it was easier working full-time because you were just constantly there and didn't have any choice."

But the full-time commitment required of a downtown practice—meaning 12- to 15-hour days—was not an option Fisher was willing to consider. "I totally missed out on my second child while he was a baby—he just grew up while I was at work. When I first started working, my daughter was in kindergarten and I didn't know anything about the school, the teachers, the principal. I just dropped her off at school and we went our separate ways. I couldn't do that again."

Fisher began to toy with the idea of going off on her own. But the prospect of starting a firm from scratch seemed too daunting a task to undertake herself. She decided to approach Schirmer with the plan. Both liked the idea of having the emotional, as well as financial, support of partners who shared their vision of a workplace that accommodated and encouraged a life beyond the office. They saw the firm itself as a modern-day version of the traditional storefront legal office that served the people of the surrounding community with reasonable rates and a personalized touch. Their big-firm experience would give them an impressive edge, they reasoned, and if they could set up shop closer to their suburban homes, they would be able to cut out the commute and cut down on costs.

For Schirmer, it was a role that finally made sense. "The control, the flexibility and the work itself—having clients that I could relate to, not some huge multimillion-dollar accounts—it was exactly what I had been looking for." The two colleagues hooked up with Cheryl Berdelle, a former classmate of Schirmer's who handled criminal appeals for the Illinois appellate defender's office, and started plotting.

The three women would meet discreetly in dark downtown restaurants during lunch hours, not wanting to tip off their employers until they were sure they could pull it off. The toughest part of their several months of behind-the-scenes planning turned out to be finding an appropriate and affordable office space. Their first priority was to eliminate the downtown commute. That meant locating a space in Oak Park, where Fisher and Schirmer live. Berdelle lives just ten minutes away in nearby Riverdale. Although the average rents of $1,200 to $2,000 a month were lower than they would have been downtown, they were not practical for a new firm with an uncertain client base and a start-up budget that consisted of $5,000 from each of the women's savings accounts.

After four months of scouring real-estate ads, perusing downtown office buildings for unadvertised deals and spending weekends and nights walking the streets with a local realtor, the women stumbled onto their current space on the ground floor of an old landmark condominium building, a few blocks from the train station. "It was a total pit," says Fisher. It also cost less than half the going market rate. The offices had previously been occupied by a rubber tire union. Asbestos tiles hung from the ceiling. Fluorescent light fixtures dangled from metal poles. The old carpeting had water damage. The walls were covered with rotting cork board. No one had painted the place in years. The three women decided to take it. They negotiated a deal in which they would pay about $200 more in rent each month in exchange for the building managers agreeing to clean up and renovate the space. On June 1, 1988, they opened for business.

The original plan was to work four days a week. But the demands of starting a new business and building a solid client base made that impossible. Today, the women typically work five days a week but maintain a very reasonable nine-to-five schedule. The work has also turned out to be more challenging than they had anticipated. Says Fisher: "In our old firm, Robin and I did real-estate transactions exclusively. In a small office, though, you can't have such a narrow practice. If someone calls up and says they need a will done, you can't just turn it down because you're not an estate planner. We have really had to work hard to educate ourselves in areas that we had little experience in before. Even though we're not working on the multimillion-dollar deals anymore, in some ways it is just as interesting and much tougher."

Even with the inevitable stresses that come from building a business from scratch, all three women say their lives are simpler and more satisfying. "I love the fact that I'm not spending an hour each way commuting," says Schirmer who now lives six blocks from the office. "That's what I've really gained in terms of being able to spend more time with my child." For Fisher, full-time self-employment is far less stressful than part-time on a traditional track. "I can take a short break in the middle of the day to go meet with the principal and not feel this constant anxiety that I should be checking in with the office. Even if I have to come in for a few hours occasionally on the weekends it doesn't feel like work—it's all just part of the natural flow of my life."

Fisher has also worked to maintain her professional/social network by meeting people from her old firm for lunch when she is downtown on business. But she admits that her life now is more isolating. In some ways, Fisher says, she feels a little like an outsider—not quite part of the professional mainstream, but also removed from the world of stay-at-home mothers. "Last summer, when I was taking my then five-year-old to baseball practice, it became clear to me that there was this whole social network of mothers. They all knew each other and would bring blankets and food for a picnic, and make a whole day of these events. I felt a little marginal, like I didn't exactly fit in because the most I could do was come and watch the game and then quickly get back to the office." In a sense, what pioneers like Fisher, Schirmer and Berdelle are doing is inventing a new middle ground approach to the family/career dilemma. As suburban self-employers they must carve out a role that falls somewhere in between that of the stay-at-home mother and the full-time urban worker. With few models to show them the way, however, that isn't always easy.

Having the support and camaraderie of a group partnership has helped ease the sense of isolation and detachment from the larger professional mainstream. Furthermore, having the resources and diverse backgrounds of three individuals to fall back on has softened the pressures of bringing in new business. Berdelle, for instance, has been able to get client referrals from her father, a lawyer himself who also worked for many years as a solo practitioner. Schirmer and Fisher have taken advantage of contacts at their old firm. "Essentially we took a leap of faith when we started up," says Fisher. "Each of us came from five or six years of legal experience and we just felt that we had enough connections to get the business we needed to get going."

Unlike partners in a large firm who have already built up their own client base, Fisher and Schirmer essentially left their old jobs emptyhanded. Even so, their former employer has pitched in to help. About half the women's initial business came from handling house closings for employees and clients of the old firm. The service, offered by the law firm free of charge to employees, used to be handled in-house by attorneys in their spare time. Berdelle, Schirmer and Fisher are now paid a flat fee to do it. They have also attracted work by getting articles written about them in local newspapers and through friends, family and former colleagues who refer clients generally for real-estate closings and estate planning. "Most of the work we get now is for people who are essentially at our level of life. Before we were so removed from the clients that it never seemed real," says Fisher. "It feels good to be working for people who need our services and are really happy about what we do for them."

More than other downshifters, most self-employed people will need to be prepared for a significant drop in income—at least initially. "We walked away from a lot of money and I seriously doubt we will ever come close to making that much again," says Fisher. "This was definitely more of a lifestyle decision than a money-making one." Schirmer, for instance, whose husband makes a relatively modest income as a legal-aid attorney, saw her salary drop from over $80,000 a year to "something that doesn't register on an EKG." But she says the toughest part has been adjusting psychologically to having less. For the first time in years Schirmer has had to learn to think before spending. "When I'm standing at a parking meter and it gives me a choice of a nickel or a dime, I use the nickel now," says Schirmer, who insists that the overall quality of her life has not been dramatically affected by her lower income. "Before we would just buy without thinking. Now we are a little less free with fast-spending dollars."

But the couple has made some lifestyle adjustments: They traded in their two Mazdas for one Toyota station wagon, and as an extra cushion regularly sign up for free lines of credit offered through the mail by banks and credit card companies. Schirmer also isn't timid about clipping coupons. "I think the way we are spending money now is much healthier," she says.

For Fisher, whose current income is actually lower than

her part-time salary at the Chicago firm, the biggest change has been learning to live without upward mobility. She and her husband Larry, who is in marketing research, have put off buying the larger house they had been planning on. Instead, the couple live very economically, just six minutes from Fisher's office, in a two-flat Victorian with a tenant on the first floor. Fisher has not so much cut back her spending as plateaued her lifestyle. "I think sometimes that it would be nice to have my own house with a back door off the kitchen and no tenant downstairs, but it is certainly not such a priority that I would give up all the control and freedom over my life that this job has brought me."

Subcontracting: on your own but not alone

Part of the appeal of a group arrangement is that it offers a happy medium for those accustomed to working in a more disciplined corporate setting. In a similar way, subcontracting can provide a bridge between pure entrepreneurship and a confining corporate career. Some self-employers even continue to work for their previous employers, performing tasks similar to a full-time employee but under the slightly altered role of consultant or subcontractor.

This vast and evolving segment of the work force now represents 40 percent of all employment in the business service industry, according to a 1989 study by the National Planning Association. The growth has occurred as both expanding and downsizing companies search for more efficient methods of maintaining a work force. The NPA study gave the example of one company whose total number of consultants and temporary workers grew from 1 or 2 percent in 1980 to 27 percent in 1987. Approximately two-thirds of those workers were consultants and one-third were full-time temporary employees. The report found that a key reason for the increase was that many of the most talented individuals in their fields preferred the flexibility of consulting arrangements.

Even so, because of the huge glut of so-called consultants during the past decade, this form of self-employment has developed something of a bad name. Many consultants in the 1980s seemed to fit into two extremes. There was the upper-level manager, grabbing the brass ring of early retirement, escaping from the corporate rat race and insisting that he was going to be a consultant. A few letters may have gone out, probably business cards were printed up, but in reality he spent little time consulting and a lot of time on the golf course. On the other end of the spectrum was the young free-lancer. Usually a recent college graduate rebelling against the strictures of the corporate career track, he or she hustled for every penny, scrounged for every assignment and occasionally even earned a living after several years of building contacts and gaining respect.

The downshifting self-employer is ahead of both types in several important ways. Unlike the golf-course consultant, the downshifter still needs to earn a living and is a long way from retirement. For every ex-corporate honcho who merely uses the title "consultant" as a convenient substitute for "early retiree," there are dozens of others who are winning big assignments and making substantial contributions. Likewise, a 35-year-old former fast-tracker setting up his or her own shop has little if anything in common with a 24-year-old free-lancer struggling to make ends meet. The downshifter has already spent several years in the work force and is likely to have a network of professional resources to tap into.

There are, of course, tradeoffs for those who choose the subcontracting route. The most obvious is the lack of security if a project runs out of funds or assignments become scarce. But what is lost in job security may be more than made up for in flexibility. Subcontractors are free to set their own hours and create a work environment that is far removed from the pressures and politics of a corporate career track. Because they establish a relationship with one or two primary clients—frequently their former employer—they also eliminate one of the most stressful elements of self-employment: the need to constantly sell themselves to bring in new business and generate income.

Subcontracting is often a more manageable alternative to part-time staff positions, especially for those whose job descriptions or personalities would make it difficult to set limits on a traditional career track. Mary Ann Oven found that what was considered impossible while she was still on the payroll as a full-time employee of Chase Manhattan Bank in international operations management was remarkably simple when she switched her official role from "employee" to "subcontractor." "After I came back from maternity leave, the personnel department had no interest in helping me pursue alternative career arrangements such as a flexible schedule or part-time work," says Oven, who had just given birth to her first child. So Oven, a second vice-president at the time, took matters into her own hands. She conducted what she describes as a "mini mass-marketing campaign" throughout the bank, sending out 40 resumes and cover letters explaining that she was looking for part-time work. The search resulted in one "enlightened" vice-president offering her a consulting assignment. Oven quit her job at the bank, and, in December 1985, assumed the role of subcontractor.

During her first four years of working as a consultant for Chase, Oven only had to compete for one out of a total of eight assignments. "This arrangement almost completely eliminates the need to sell myself," says Oven, whose projects have included writing a comprehensive procedures manual for the bank on international securities. Oven worked on the two-year-long project three days a week, splitting her time between her Flemington, New Jersey, home, where she writes and does revisions on her personal computer, and the bank's New York offices, where she conducts interviews and gathers data. Although Oven, who now has two young children, would like to continue the arrangement indefinitely, she admits that the lack of security can be troubling. "I know that they could cut me out of the budget at any time. A few weeks ago the manager on the project I'm working on told me that he had to justify my presence and paycheck to his new boss. Those things can't help but make you feel a little insecure."

It is possible to erase some of that uncertainty—but again, there are tradeoffs. When Diane Davis Reed first considered self-employment, she was leery of putting herself into yet another unstable situation. In the past 13 years, Reed, who had been a human resources manager in the retail and banking industries, had felt the sharp jolt and rippling aftershocks of corporate mergers so many times that conducting job searches—whether for herself or for those she counseled after their jobs were eliminated—was becoming her foremost specialty. Following her third company merger and second layoff, Reed decided it was time to put her evolving skills to use in a more productive and positive manner.

Although going off on her own seemed the best solution, the recently remarried Kansas City woman in her mid-40s wanted to avoid adding more tumult to her life after so many years of living with corporate upheaval. She also wanted to get away from the time-consuming administrative duties that had bogged her down in her previous jobs and prevented her from focusing on her counseling work. Her solution, a twist on the subcontracting theme, was to piggyback on to a larger, better-established firm.

During her own job searches in the past, Reed had been in contact with a well-known local group called the Career Management Center. She thought that if she could hook up with such a group, she would eliminate many of the administrative duties of running her own show, while gaining control over the type of work she did and when she did it. As it happened, Career Management Center was interested in setting up a contracting arrangement with a human resources professional who could conduct job search seminars for corporate level executives. Reed was able to strike an agreement in which she would use the center's offices and staff in exchange for giving up a percentage of the income she brings in through her consulting work. "It is like having my own business, but I don't have to manage it as much. I don't have to worry about paying bills, or hiring a support staff or getting the Xerox machine fixed," says Reed. She also can take advantage of the center's established name and reputation for joint marketing efforts.

Although Reed has had to give up some of the financial rewards that would come from being totally independent, she believes she has more control under this arrangement than if she had gone off completely on her own. Under her current agreement with Career Management Center, Reed gets 50 to 60 percent of the clients' fees she brings in, in exchange for the center handling all of the administrative work and providing her with office space.

Although her gross income, as a result, is about half what it had been under her previous employer, Reed has been able to cut down on expenses significantly simply by being her own boss and no longer having to maintain an image of corporate success. "Little things, like being able to bring my own lunch every day, have really made a difference. When you are part of upper management in an organization—especially when you are the only woman in the management group—you just don't

brownbag. It wasn't acceptable, and things like that are unfortu-
nately important when you are trying to fit in and not seem too
different." The cost of Reed's executive wardrobe has also been
reduced dramatically as she has forgone suits for much less
expensive skirts and sweaters. In general, however, Reed says
she feels less of a compulsion to spend money. "The happier I
am, the less money I spend. I am just much more satisfied with
my life."

Reed typically works a 35- to 50-hour week—similar to her
former jobs—but far less than the workaholic lifestyle typical of
many entrepreneurs trying to get a business off the ground. More
than a reduction in hours, however, what most self-employers
are looking for is flexibility. "I don't take appointments before
nine in the morning and don't come in before ten if I don't have
anyone to see. I always liked having the mornings to myself to
exercise or meditate or just putter around, but when you have
to make it into the office by eight or eight-thirty every morning
that is pretty difficult. Little things like that add to this overall
sense of freedom I now have."

The temp option: independence without the risk

Achieving the autonomy of the entrepreneur and balance of the
downshifter requires, as we have seen, taking creative approaches to self-employment. The fact is, starting a business is
typically no time to be setting limits. Just getting a new enterprise
off the ground can be a seven-day-a-week, 24-hour-a-day preoc-
cupation. As a result, some of the options used by downshifters
may not seem like what we have traditionally come to think of
as self-employment. A good example is temporary employment.
Once reserved for recent college grads and unemployed clerical

workers, more professionals are finding temping a relatively risk-free alternative to striking out completely on their own.

In 1988, according to the National Association of Temporary Services (NATS), U.S. businesses spent $9.9 billion on temporary help, employing an average of approximately one million temps a day, more than double the 1983 figures of $4 billion and 471,000 workers. The fastest-growing group in this segment are professional temps. It is estimated that at least 17 percent of the temporary work force is made up of managerial, professional, technical or skilled blue-collar workers. "Many of these are people who just don't want to play the corporate game any more and who are looking for a more reasonable quality of life," says Samuel Sacco, executive vice-president of NATS. The result has been a gradual lifting of the stigma attached to temping as a last resort for people who can't find a job. "When you have doctors and lawyers working as temps, there is less of a tendency to look down on it."

Clearly, flexibility is the primary motivator for full-time professionals switching to temporary work. Growing labor shortages in the service sector give temps the luxury of choosing who they will work for, when they will work, when they will take time off and what industries they will concentrate on. A manager who finds himself out on the street after a corporate downsizing and wants to test his options before diving back into the rat race can hook up with any of a number of firms throughout the country, such as Klivan, Becker and Smith in Cleveland and Interim Management Company in New York, which match up executives in areas such as finance, manufacturing and marketing on a temporary basis. A scientist searching for more flexibility than is typically offered in a full-time corporate setting could sign on with Lab Support, Inc. in Woodland Hills, California, a so-called rent-a-chemist operation that places scientists for project-oriented work in industrial, environmental and biotechnology labs.

On the down side, what temps gain in flexibility they may lose in control while they are on the job. "As a temporary worker, what you don't get to choose is the duration of an assignment or the way it will be carried out," notes Eve Broudy in *Professional Temping*. In a typical temporary arrangement, "you are expected to conform to a company's work codes and standards and, because time is invaluable, you are also expected to dive in and give your top performance from day one."[3] There is also the element of uncertainty to contend with: A long-term assignment could fizzle out after only a few days if a client suddenly changes his needs. You may also have to foot the bill for your own medical benefits and other perks associated with full-time employment, although some temporary firms are starting to offer benefits packages to professionals.

In general, however, professional temps enjoy most of the freedoms associated with subcontractors, consultants and freelancers, with one major plus: their paychecks come from one steady source, the temporary employment agency that finds them work. The firm typically bills the client company for the temporary employee's services on a daily or hourly basis and then pays the employee a percentage of that sum. For downshifters anxious to separate themselves from the daily pressures and responsibilities that come with membership in the community of work, professional temping can provide a steady stream of challenging assignments and a reliable income source.

Matthew Lind, an engineer with a doctorate in applied mathematics, is typical of the new breed of professionals turning to temporary work as a vehicle for downshifting their careers and gaining more autonomy over their professional lives. Lind's impressive credentials included a stint during the Ford and Carter administrations as head of the Pension Benefit Guaranty Corporation and, more recently, a group presidency at Mutual Life Insurance of New York, where he oversaw all noninsurancerelated business and drew an annual income of about $400,000. Despite his success, however, Lind was extremely unhappy with the overall quality of his life.

On the professional end, like many career climbers, his success had propelled him into work that held little value or interest for him—even though it garnered him a great deal of power, respect and financial rewards. "I have always enjoyed the creative and technical side of financial analysis, but I was spending most of my time traveling to subsidiaries or sitting in meetings where a lot of time and energy was wasted on political battles," says Lind, who is now in his late 40s.

On a personal level, the combination of being on the road 60 to 80 percent of the time and forcing himself to do a job he found unsatisfying had turned him into, in his words, "an irritable and not very nice person. I was angry a lot because it felt like everyone wanted a piece of my flesh. During vacations at our summer place I would spend half the time on the phone conducting business and generally pissing everyone off—my family, myself and my colleagues." Lind shut out friends and ignored for several years a number of outside passions, including sports and music. "I walked around with this pain in my chest. I felt like I was disappointing everyone, especially myself."

Despite his unhappiness, making a break wasn't easy. Beyond the income, Lind had grown accustomed to the influence of his position and the perks that came with it—the glamour imagery that was as much a part of his job as the actual work he did. "I was surprised because I never saw myself as someone who was caught up in the trappings of the job. But when you are in a position like that you really are the king of your little world. Even things like giving up the limousines was difficult." Lind's initial solution was to go the straight entrepreneurial route, where, he believed, the thrill of being his own boss and doing the type of work he enjoyed most would make the loss of status seem less significant. He hooked up with friends who were forming a small investment banking firm, Stratmore Group, specializing in mortgage banking. As a co-owner of the firm he assigned himself the role of "technical expert."

Almost immediately, Lind's life changed dramatically—perhaps too dramatically. He worked from his home in New Rochelle, New York, doing financial analysis much of the day on his personal computer. "I loved not having to travel so much or do client development and hand-holding, but my life went from one extreme to another." Like many professionals who start working at home after years in the professional urban mainstream, Lind had a hard time adjusting to the isolation and detachment, not to mention the financial uncertainties of owning a new business. "I went from an existence where I was never home and under constant stress to one where I was home all the time. Although I was doing work I enjoyed and developing new skills, I felt like a college student again, sitting at home in my dungarees and having minimal contact with the outside world." By upgrading his old IBM, Lind had also managed to cut his technical work for Stratmore in half, and had time to explore new opportunities. He was beginning to feel too that between paying his daughter's college bills and meeting alimony payments for his first marriage, he was going to require a more steady income than could be counted on from Stratmore, which had suffered some economic setbacks.

He knew about the temporary employment option from a former professional associate who was president of Interim Management Company and felt it would offer the security and autonomy he was looking for—as well as an opportunity to be in an office again. Within weeks of contacting Interim, Lind was dispatched to USGI, a Darien, Connecticut-based mortgage service outfit, which needed someone to oversee new corporate development following the departure of a company executive who had previously headed those operations. Management of the 100-employee company did not want to risk hurting morale again by hiring another full-time vice-president who might not have worked out, and was also uncertain how long the position would be required.

Lind's arrangement called for USGI to pay the temp firm $2,250 a day—$1,500 of which went to him. Even without benefits, Lind, who was working just four days a week and continuing to put in some time for Stratmore, felt it was a good deal. What's more, his position as director of corporate development allowed him to do the creative planning and financial analysis he enjoyed, while being completely removed from the energy-depleting politics of the corporate bureaucracy. After several months of working on a temporary basis, Lind was asked and accepted an offer to work for USGI on a full-time basis. "Temping allowed me to get a taste of what was in store before I plunged into something again," says Lind. Before accepting USGI's offer, however, Lind made certain that his role would not change. In fact, Lind says, his current situation maintains many of the attributes of temporary employment. He works at home one or two days a week, giving him more time to spend with his wife and infant son. He also has made a point of positioning himself outside the all-consuming community of work. "I have no one reporting to me. Instead, I am like an in-house consultant who people seek out when they need problems solved or advice on particular issues. I am not saddled with meetings or involved in internal politics. What I have done is taken real control of my life."

Lind feels he has achieved the perfect balance. "My work and home life are more integrated than ever. I can get up early in the morning and work at home or put in a few hours on the weekend, and I don't feel I'm disappointing my family or missing out on activities I want to get involved in." However, because his professional and home life are so seamless now, Lind makes a point of setting limits for himself. When working at home he sets daily goals and considers the work day done once they have been met. He also takes time out for leisure activities during the day, including playing tennis or taking occasional 15-minute breaks to play the piano. His life, he says, is "very civilized." Even when he goes into the office, his commute is an easy 25 minutes and he is usually home by 5 p.m. "When I think now about how I used to leave my home for my office in Manhattan at six a.m. and not start heading back until after seven p.m., I just think it was inhuman. It was completely unnecessary."

More professionals who also once blindly accepted long commutes and urban-centered success imagery are beginning to respond in much the same way as Lind. As we have seen with other downshifters, such as Ken Bode, who left his job at NBC News in Washington, D.C., for a university position in a small Indiana town, these professionals are questioning the assumption that one must live in an expensive, gridlocked urban world in order to pursue a successful career. Part of the appeal of self-employment is that it typically allows professionals to set up shop where they please. But entrepreneurs aren't the only ones who can benefit from the simpler lifestyles found outside of major urban centers. For growing numbers of back-trackers, career shifters and plateauers, reinventing success means living in a smaller city or town where a successful family and community life is often more important than achievement in a career.

7

· ·

The Urban Escapee

"I went to the woods because I wished to live deliberately, to front only the essential facts of life, and see if I could not learn what it had to teach, and not, when I came to die, discover that I had not lived."

—Henry David Thoreau, 1854[1]

"We went to the country with nothing but our city furniture. We began by adding to this wholly unsuitable equipment for pioneering an electric range. This was the first purchase in the long list of domestic machines with which we proposed to test our theory that it was possible to be more comfortable in the country than in the city, with security, independence, and freedom to do the work to which we aspired thrown in for good measure."

— Ralph Borsodi, 1920,
former marketing consultant for
Macy's department store[2]

"All of us are city people; we learn by doing. With a book in one hand, seeds in the other, and a kind of optimism, we grow most of our own food. We have no electricity, no telephone, no running water, no tractor. We do have a car and a truck that runs sometimes, but not so many bills and as little dependency on the industrial-technocracy as we can now manage. We dig living this way . . . "
— *Patsy (Richardson) Sun, a member of the Freefolk commune in Minnesota during the late 1960s*[3]

"We moved to rural Minnesota for all the hackneyed reasons, to be near beauty, quiet and animals. But we are real technopeasants. We have three bathrooms and two computers. It was never part of the plan to come here and live off the land. We didn't want to change who we were, just where we lived."
— *Patty Feld, 1989, former choreographer and director of the Minnesota Opera Company*[4]

Throughout history, Americans have sought refuge in the peace and serenity of the countryside, devising their own schemes for achieving a better life. From Henry David Thoreau on Walden Pond to the "turn on, tune in, drop out" hippies of the 1960s and the "technopeasants" of the 1980s combining computers with wood-burning stoves, an idyllic country life, free of the pressures of urban insanity, has always had romantic appeal. What such lifestyle alternatives have rarely provided, however, is a realistic and workable model for living, thriving and raising a family in a modern world. "For the most part, massive shifts toward simplicity such as the back-to-the-land movements have had a very short life span," notes David E. Shi, who has written several books on the simple life. "People looking for an overnight conversion are bound to be disappointed and will inevitably backslide to the old way."

The mass exodus of fed-up yuppies to the quaint country inns of New England is a stunning recent example of this problem. In the past decade, the number of commercial bed and breakfasts and country inns grew by more than 200 percent, with an estimated 20,000 such establishments now operating primarily on the East and West coasts. On the surface, running a B&B would seem to offer everything worn-out fast-trackers are looking for: the opportunity to get away from the urban rat race while still building a business and meeting interesting people.

The reality, however, of making ends meet in the world of quilts and pine furniture often leaves B&B owners feeling that they have merely replaced one rat race with another. There are no concrete figures on just how many B&Bs change hands or go out of business, but Sallie Clark, executive director of Bed and Breakfast Innkeepers of Colorado, estimates that the average B&B owner calls it quits after one to two years. "It is usually impossible to see any return until after the fourth year and most people just haven't prepared themselves either emotionally or financially to stick it out that long," says Clark. Those who do make it almost always rely on at least one full-time outside income beyond the B&B operation. A study of B&Bs in Colorado revealed that only 14 percent of the establishments' owners used them as a sole source of income; 51 percent said the inns provided less than 40 percent of their total household income.

What the B&B phenomenon and other similar mass movements to the country do tell us, however, is that people are searching, no matter how awkwardly, for options beyond cookie-cutter urban professionalism. An underlying theme seems to fuel most urban escapees: It is a belief that the high prices, honking horns and impatient tenor of urban and suburban life have pushed them further and further away from the sense of neighborhood and community found in smalltown America. "People feel a very tenuous connection with the places they live in and little control over their environment," says Elizabeth Plater-Zyberk, a Miami architect who, in an effort to recapture some of that community spirit, has helped design several suburban villages across the country modeled after traditional American towns.

Smalltown life, however, has more than philosophical appeal. As average home prices in the past decade climbed past the $200,000 mark in many cities, the prospect of building a reasonable life in metropolitan America became increasingly remote. Even for well-paid professionals, the possibility of simply finding an affordable house was often incentive enough to transplant the family to a distant outpost of the rural Midwest. When a story appeared in the national media in 1988 that Rolfe, Iowa, a town of 700, was offering a free building lot and $1,200 to anyone who would come to live there, more than 5,000 letters poured in from such pricey spots as Massachusetts, Connecticut and New Jersey.

In fact, during the upwardly mobile era of the 1980s urban professional, the two fastest-growing slices of America were actually the outermost suburbs or exurbs and gentrifying rural counties, classified as "retirement communities" because at least 15 percent of their population growth in the 1970s came from people 60 and older. In recent years, however, retirees have accounted for only part of that growth. These approximately 500 counties, scattered across the country from Florida to New England to the Upper Great Lakes and the Pacific Northwest, are typically near or part of popular recreation spots where professionals have bought second homes or participated in summer shares. They are now moving into those homes year-round.

Wayne County, Pennsylvania, for example, located in the Pocono Mountains and encompassing several popular lakes, saw its population grow by 14.9 percent between 1980 and 1988 to 40,500 as refugees flooded in from the high-priced, high-stress New York/New Jersey corridor. Overall, the population of these nonmetropolitan counties increased 15 percent between 1980 and 1988 to a total of 13.4 million compared with a 9.7 percent growth for metropolitan areas and a 4.7 percent increase in rural America. As the populations of retirement counties have grown, so have professional opportunities. "The younger people that are moving in are maintaining professional-level careers by either starting their own businesses or joining small service businesses," says Calvin Beale, senior demographer for the U.S. Department of Agriculture.

For such individuals, downshifting is often a matter of simply finding a less stressful environment to pursue their careers. There is no question that expectations about careers and emphasis on work are much greater in some areas of the country than they are in others. Most notably, the big cities of the East Coast, which attract a large percentage of young professionals, are far more focused on career status and macho workaholism than even comparable cities in the Midwest and on the West Coast. An advertising executive in New York, for example, is likely to work well into the evenings most days and on weekends at a typical medium to large firm. At a comparable Seattle shop, on the other hand, the executive would make it home most evenings to have dinner with the family, as well as have weekends free for hiking, biking and sailing.

Such differences reflect not only varying notions about work but divergent attitudes about time and leisure. Psychologist Robert Levine of California State University in Fresno points out that different regions and even cities have their own "distinct

175

rhythms and rules. Seemingly simple words like 'now,' snapped out by an impatient New Yorker, and 'later,' said by a relaxed Californian, suggest a world of difference."[5] The classically laid-back attitudes and generally easier lifestyles found in smaller cities may be one reason for the recent population surge in such areas as Phoenix, Arizona; Charlotte, North Carolina; Albuquerque, New Mexico; and Fort Worth, Texas. These cities were growth leaders between 1980 and 1988 while large urban centers like New York, Chicago and Boston experienced relatively minor population increases.

Of course, moving from Chicago to Charlotte is not quite the same as trading big-city life for a rustic cabin on an isolated mountaintop. When it comes right down to it, however, most of us have no interest in forsaking everything we have worked for to live out a romantic ideal in the woods. What we do long for is a middle ground: a place where the modern conveniences and intellectual and professional challenges of big-city life do not take us over but merely give our lives depth; where the cost of living does not force us to give up our own happiness to meet a monthly mortgage payment; and where success has a more personal meaning than continually moving ahead in a job.

Building a career in vacation paradise

Even at first glance, there are subtle, but unmistakable, clues of Jerry Vest's former life. There is the understated strand of pearls around her neck and the matching gold and pearl earrings. There is her thick blond hair pulled back conservatively from her ruddy, mountain-tanned face. There is the way she sits upright, stockinged legs crossed, hands folded confidently across her chest as if she is waiting to get down to business.

None of this would be particularly noteworthy if Vest still lived in Washington, D.C., where she once worked as a button-down mathematician for the CIA. It is the surrounding scene that makes Vest's professional appearance seem slightly out of sync. It is the mountain bikes scattered around the conference room where we are sitting. It is the fresh August breeze blowing through an open window. It is the view of a creamy white cloud, passing over and momentarily obliterating a nearby mountain peak.

Breckenridge, Colorado, is not the sort of place where people typically pursue careers—unless their ambition is to operate a ski lift, drive a mountain bus or become a member of the U.S. Ski Team. It isn't, that is, unless you are Jerry Vest.

In the summer of 1980, at the age of 30, Vest left a grueling routine of juggling graduate school with her high-pressure CIA job to spend some time with friends in the Colorado Rockies, skiing, hiking and reassessing her life. She never went back. Vest accepted what was, at the time, a relatively low-level position as a statistician for Summit County, an area that includes Brecken-ridge and several other ski resorts. She met and married her husband, Bill Burton, a partner in a chain of ski rental and retail stores, started a family and built a life and a career for herself in a spot so idyllic that Vest says hardly a day goes by when "I don't thank my lucky stars that I get to look at these mountains when-ever I feel like it."

But Jerry Vest is no dropout. She has not forsaken her career to live the life of a ski bum; nor has she pursued the narrow romantic vision of a former fast-tracker trying to make ends meet operating a quaint bed and breakfast. Instead, Vest has turned what could have been a mundane smalltown govern-ment job as county statistician into a rewarding and challenging career that includes putting together a comprehensive statistical abstract for the fast-growing area, detailing everything from population projections to retail sales to housing prices, and acting as a research and information source for new development. Says Vest: "This is certainly not the high-powered kind of position I could have if I was in Washington or New York or San Francisco. But it is a reasonable and rewarding compromise between that sort of life and dropping out. It allows me to live in one of the most beautiful places in the world and do work that I enjoy and which benefits the community."

Most urbanized professionals would be quick to dismiss people like Vest as a rare exception to an intractable rule. The refrain goes something like this: Having a real career means working in a concrete jungle of smog and traffic. The alternative, living amid beauty and nature, means either dropping out completely or suffering through a horrendously long commute every day. Vest begs to differ. "We do get very well educated people here who drop out from stressful careers for a year or two and make six dollars an hour pushing chair lifts. But the majority of full-time residents are working every day in real-life jobs and pursuing interesting careers. People think that there is just one way to have a career and that a certain kind of life must go with it. I know that that is not the case."

Acquiring such knowledge, however, didn't come easily for Vest. She was a product of the rigid professionalism churned out of big universities and a suburban upbringing and expectations. Like the rest of her peers, Vest never imagined that there might be another way to measure success. She had been recruited by the CIA in her senior year at the University of Delaware, and, throughout her ten-year career in Washington, D.C., defined her world by her job. During the two years before moving to Colorado, she endured a grueling night-shift schedule at the agency where she interpreted photographs received by satellite in the middle of the night. That typically meant coming into work at 11 p.m. or 3 a.m. and not leaving until 7:30 a.m. or

1:30 p.m. For much of that time, during her off-hours, Vest was also working toward a master's degree in economics.

Between her 45-minute commute from her home in Mount Vernon, Virginia, and an almost total absence of free time in the evenings or on weekends, Vest's world was reduced to the narrow confines of her consuming job. "There was this sense we had of being important people in an important city doing an important job. You just didn't question it." Besides, Vest's night-shift duties would be over at the end of two years and she would be able to return to a reasonably normal schedule. As it turned out, however, the agency had other plans. Recruiting professionals to work the unappealing night shift had proven more difficult than anticipated. When Vest's two-year stint was over, she and her co-workers were informed that their night schedules would be extended indefinitely.

Vest decided she had had enough. "I was totally exhausted and started to realize how little control I had over my own destiny. I was so burnt out that I knew I had to take a break to figure out what to do next." But she also realized that merely switching jobs wouldn't be enough. Much of the unhappiness and stress she was feeling was the result of living in a city where people worshiped power like a religion and where workaholism was considered an admirable quality. Vest decided that the only way to get perspective in her life was to make a total switch—not only in her job but in her living environment.

It is important to keep in mind, of course, that escaping a stressful urban life may mean different things to different people. When I left New York a few years back for Washington, D.C., I actually felt like something of an urban escapee myself. Rents were half what they had been in Manhattan and the pace of life, at least compared with claustrophobic New York subways and shoulder-to-shoulder midtown crowds, seemed almost serene. Despite the initial sense of freedom that comes from "dropping out," one of the reasons professionals who head for the country inns of Vermont often feel dissatisfied is that they have gone too far. After several years of living in big-city pressure-cooker environments, what they really want is a more manageable lifestyle, not complete isolation and detachment from everything they have valued and worked for. As I found, and as we will see later in the chapter, such a balance can be achieved in a smaller city that offers a relatively slowed-down environment and strong sense of community.

In Vest's case, her social ties in Colorado, combined with a passion for outdoor sports, made her decision to head for the Rockies a logical choice. When Vest first left Washington, her initial plan was to use the money she had saved by working long hours and having minimal outside life to essentially take an extended vacation in Colorado. But Vest soon realized she could never sustain herself emotionally, intellectually or materially in an environment that did not allow her to express her innate drive to succeed in some way. "I consider myself an ambitious person," she says. She missed the sense of satisfaction she had always felt from working hard and doing well in a job. She saw the county statistician's job listed in the newspaper, and thought it would at least allow her to apply her background in statistics and numbers. "I didn't even bother applying for anything else. I figured even though it was sort of underemployment at the time, it would at least keep me busy until I decided what to do next."

Quickly, however, it became clear to Vest that the job had more potential than she had initially imagined. From 1970 to 1980, Summit was the fastest-growing county in the country, with a 232 percent population increase. With investors, bankers and developers flocking into the area, Vest felt there was an obvious need for a central resource of sophisticated statistical information. "In the past, the statistician had basically just kept records of building permits and population growth. It was never expected that the person in this job would have the ability to analyze the statistics as well." Vest used her advanced skills to add a new level of sophistication to the job, and set out to develop a detailed statistical abstract of the county. The 175-page book is now produced annually, with quarterly updates. Additionally, whenever a new project is being planned, Vest is there to provide the statistical analysis for such items as sewer and water projections and to act as a spokesperson for the county.

In response to her successes, the county commissioners have had to devise a promotion track for Vest, moving her up within the ranks of the planning department since there is no career track in the statistical department—she is it. "Certainly my work at the CIA was much more critical in that if I messed up I was in deep, deep trouble. But here I am the only person responsible for what I am doing. I am not part of a team—it is totally up to me to make this department work and in many ways that is more of a challenge." The job also gives her a sense of connecting with the community in a way that was impossible while she was in Washington, where her work was classified and there was virtually no public contact. "In this job, I am always going out talking about the local economy to the Rotary Club and various development groups. There is a feeling of helping people in a concrete way. Every time I talk to them I get instant feedback."

But in the world Vest now lives in, it would be impossible to fall into a lifestyle that was totally consumed by career. Just outside the red brick courthouse building where she works, a field of poppies bends westward toward the deep green mountain peaks. On this cool August day, hikers make their way up lush mountain trails and bike enthusiasts assert themselves against the misty wind. "Your priorities change," says Vest. "You may have the ambition to work and do well at what you do, but it isn't the priority it once was." In Vest's office, no one thinks twice about taking two hours off to go skiing during lunch, and then making the time up by working later that evening. "I was just back east visiting recently and found it utterly amazing how differently people approach the whole notion of recreation. I have this friend in D.C. who was really into bike riding and used to ride around the city all the time. But he was always getting hit by cars. Someone was always knocking him off his bike."

When Vest decided to transplant her life to the Colorado Rockies, however, she knew that she would need more than pretty surroundings or even an interesting job to feel satisfied. She was also looking for a place that would satisfy her desire to meet and befriend vital and stimulating people who shared her cultural, social and intellectual interests. A resort community attracting a range of highly educated and involved people from around the world proved to be the perfect compromise. "It was so easy to make friends and meet people here—you feel this automatic bond. When I came to Washington it probably took me a good year before I had a close circle of friends. Here the community is smaller and people are more open. There is also a more diverse cross-section of artsy and very interesting people," says the extremely extroverted Vest. Because of the heavy emphasis on cultural and recreational activities often found in resort towns, professionals may find the social atmosphere even more friendly and open than traditional small towns and cities where activities are often centered around tight-knit neighborhood and family circles.

Almost from the day she arrived, Vest was drawn into a variety of community activities, which quickly provided her with a sense of belonging she had never felt in Washington. She did volunteer work as an advocate for abused women, has been involved in fundraising activities with the Breckenridge Music Institute and is an active member of her church group. Although neither she nor her husband, who is from Salt Lake City, have family in the immediate area, their community life is so strong that it provides the couple and their two young children with many of the feelings of intimacy and connection that come from family life. "We even have a local grandma," says Vest, referring to the elderly woman who took care of both her children before they were in school and now insists on having them over to her house on a regular basis.

Vest does, however, pay a heftier financial price than most urban escapees for her decision to live in vacation paradise. While not as expensive as major cities like Washington, New York or San Francisco, the cost of living in Colorado's well-to-do mountain communities can be steep. The average price of a three- or four-bedroom home in Breckenridge, for instance, is in the $150,000 to $200,000 range, and such items as gasoline and food may actually be more expensive than in urban areas where there is more to choose from.

Vest could, of course, quickly boost her income if she was willing to give up her Colorado lifestyle. With her now-extensive computer and research expertise she would have no trouble landing a job in a big-city consulting or market research firm where her salary would increase by $20,000 overnight. Her husband as well, with his extensive retail experience, could also easily transplant his career almost anywhere in the country. But whenever the couple sit down to do the arithmetic it always comes out clearly in favor of staying put. Vest puts it simply: "There is a certain cost involved in the quality of life." And it is a cost the couple is more than willing to pay.

When going back means going home

No matter what route they ultimately decide to take, most urban escapees are motivated in large part by the need to reestablish closer ties to community and family. In some cases, as with Vest, the literal closeness to family was not so much the issue as the need to be in an environment where a sense of community, rather than individual achievements, was the central focus of life. In other instances, the retreat from large urban centers is a retreat to the comforts of home.

Studies during the past decade have shown a growing yearning on the part of urban professionals for the support and stability of the extended family life typically associated with smalltown America. In the early 1980s, social psychologist Daniel Yankelovich wrote that one of the most far-reaching changes in social norms to have emerged during the 1970s involved a shift in "what parents believe they owe their children and what their children owe them." In a series of studies on the American family, Yankelovich pointed out that a clear pattern had emerged of a dramatic softening of the parent-child bond. "Parents expect to make fewer sacrifices for their children than their parents did in the past, but they also demand less from their offspring in the form of future obligations than their parents demanded from them."

Having the freedom to distance ourselves from familial roots was part of the general movement away from traditional male and female roles. But even in the 1970s, people were already expressing a feeling that perhaps we had gone too far. Wrote Yankelovich: "Americans long for the warmth and closeness they associate with family life in earlier decades, but not if it means going back to the old rules."[6]

The vast majority of professionals today have yet to find a workable middle ground between these two needs. "Many people are clearly missing the emotional support provided by the extended family, but few are trying to remedy the situation by staying where their parents, siblings, aunts and uncles and other family members live," notes Albert Solnit of the Child Study

Center at Yale University. With the psychological support provided by the extended family typically confined to times of crisis and holidays, professionals who have moved away from home to pursue careers, especially those who are single and do not have children of their own, increasingly turn to their communities of work to give them that sense of family and security. "A lot of the support systems that were once generated by the extended family must now come from other sources—such as friends and colleagues who live and work in the same geographical area," says Solnit. "If that support isn't sufficient, people end up feeling isolated and alienated."

As we have seen throughout this book, it is easy to get so consumed by the community of work that, for a time at least, career climbers genuinely feel they need nothing else. This is reinforced by a baby boomer success imagery that has tended to equate success with "making it" in an environment that is both physically and emotionally distant from the homogeneous suburban upbringings they grew up in. "Moving back home seemed like it would be taking the easy way out," says Carolyn Bodie, a public relations executive whose vision of success had always included living and working in a glamorous urban setting, far removed from her cozy Baltimore upbringing and close family life. Like thousands of other baby boomer career climbers, Bodie set out to create a life for herself that was vastly removed from the "nice, but predictable" middle-class world she grew up in.

From the time she went away to school at the University of Virginia in Charlottesville, and then, immediately after graduating in 1978, when she headed straight for a job as an advertising assistant at a bank in Boston, Bodie pursued this vision of geographic, as well as professional, success. When she moved to New York at the age of 26 to try her hand in the cosmetics industry, it seemed like an unbeatable opportunity. Says Bodie: "A lot of little girls go through the stage of playing with their mother's makeup and fragrances. Well, I got stuck in it. I couldn't imagine anything more wonderful than making it my career." It also seemed like the perfect industry in which to pursue her emerging interest in public relations and advertising. In New York, Bodie landed a job as manager of the up-scale Georgette Klinger skin-care salon and was quickly promoted to public relations director for the entire national chain. "I was the envy of all my friends," she says.

Part of Bodie's role in a glamour profession included immersing herself in New York's cult of busyness. By nature, Bodie is highly energetic. But her New York life seemed to push her into a state of perpetual motion. She would arrive at work at 8 a.m., rarely taking time out for even a short lunch break, and not leave until 8 or 9 o'clock in the evening. Her social life was often either directly or indirectly connected to her job. She frequently spent evenings dining at the home of Georgette Klinger, the matronly head of the company, or going out with stylish men whom Klinger had introduced to her. "She was always setting me up with these glamorous, wealthy guys who would call me up at 11 o'clock on a weekday night to go see a jazz concert. It was exciting, but I felt exhausted most of the time," recalls Bodie.

Even then, like many career climbers, Bodie sensed, as she puts it, "that something was missing. There was always this underlying feeling of not really connecting and not really belonging. You feel like you're playing a role—a role you're good at. But still, it's a role." Like many young professionals who no longer have the immediate support of their extended families to fall back on, Bodie's professional life had become her family life. Close-knit family businesses like the Georgette Klinger operation can be particularly enticing to young professionals looking for meaning and community, since they promote the idea that every single employee makes a difference and contributes to the overall success—or failure—of the organization. At unusually early

ages, career climbers in such companies may be given tremendous responsibility. We saw this with back-tracker Wendy Osborn Stenzel, who found herself initiated into a management role
while still in her 20s at the then fledgling Tandem Computer—
long before she had the experience to confidently handle the job.
For both Stenzel and Bodie, proving that they deserved such
responsibility became an all-consuming passion. Their sense of
obligation to their employers virtually obliterated any real life
beyond work. Says Bodie: "I tried to cut back, but Miss Klinger
had come to count on me working long hours. I had set this
pattern for myself that seemed impossible to break out of."

As she started to feel more and more confined by her
position with Klinger, and increasingly exhausted by her demanding schedule, Bodie determined that it was time to make a
separation. With her rapidly acquired skills in public relations
and impressive resume, she easily landed a job at N.W. Ayer, an
international advertising and public relations agency based in
New York. She moved up quickly at the agency and within a short
time was promoted to account manager of the coveted DeBeers
Diamond business. "I had this great job, this exciting life," says
Bodie. "I got to wear diamonds and travel around the world and
meet interesting people."

It was the image of success Bodie had always envisioned
for herself. But more than a year into her new job, she was still
plagued by the feeling that she was skimming the surface—that
her life lacked depth and purpose. Her extensive travel schedule,
for instance, made it extremely difficult to build lasting relationships with men. "I was meeting all these interesting people but
things just always seemed to fizzle out. There was never any
continuity or real closeness."

The cumulative difficulties and stresses of her New York
lifestyle also started to take a toll. It was the little things at first
that ate at her. In retrospect, says Bodie, they were pictures of

a life that was "spinning out of control." There was the time when she emerged exhausted from her office at 10:30 p.m., where she had spent the evening frantically preparing for another overseas trip, anxious to get home quickly and try to get a decent night's sleep. But there were no cabs—anywhere. A black-tie event had just let out and, as Bodie recalls, "all these people in their tuxes and gowns were pouring onto the street and taking all the cabs." As Bodie waited at a bus stop, feeling weighted down by the exhaustion and stress, she caught the eye of someone she knew. He had just emerged in his tux from the black-tie extravaganza. "He came up to me and very nicely said 'hi,' and I just became completely unglued. I started to cry. I just felt so tired. You lose all perspective."

It was during such times that Bodie first began to seriously think about forgoing her New York career and moving home to Baltimore, where the sense of community and comforts of family were starting to seem like a wonderful dream. For a long time she pushed such thoughts out of her mind as absurd. Maintaining the image of an outwardly successful life was still vitally important to Bodie. "I would go home for Thanksgiving and have all these interesting stories to tell about traveling to Tokyo and doing these glamorous things in New York. That life was what defined me. It seemed impossible to give it up."

For Bodie, the process of clarifying her needs evolved over several years of mounting unhappiness and exhaustion. The idea of making a drastic change didn't start to seriously take hold until a particularly trying series of events about a year before she left. "I was sent to Tokyo to speak about diamonds to the Japanese press. I remember feeling extremely harried preparing for the trip, harried while I was there and jet-lagged and harried when I got back. I had also been having this long-distance relationship with a man in Detroit, but it hadn't been working out. When I got back from Tokyo I called him and said it wasn't going to work. Nothing about my life seemed to have a lasting quality to it, and even the glamorous things—like going on trips to Tokyo—had become more stressful and exhausting than fun. I never seemed to be able to get enough sleep to catch up. I wasn't dating anyone seriously, work was a drain. I started thinking, Why am I here? Why am I putting up with this? What is the point?"

The success imagery that had guided Bodie's life since she had been a teenager—the big-city nightlife, the elegant wardrobe, the world travel—slowly began to fade. Her fantasies now were of home, and family and evenings by the fire with her parents, sister and niece and nephew. In the spring of 1988, at the age of 31, Bodie got up the courage to make the break. She gave up her impressive position, high salary and long-held image of herself as a big-time public relations executive to move back home to Baltimore. "I never even considered going anywhere else. I had been to a lot of other places and felt I didn't need to do that again," says Bodie. Besides, she reasoned, Baltimore seemed to offer the perfect balance—a strong family and community life, as well as solid professional opportunities.

Like Vest, however, Bodie allowed herself to ease into the transition. With her extensive experience in the public relations field, she knew it wouldn't hurt her resume to take a few months off and carefully consider her next step. She moved into her parents' house for the summer and spent mornings interviewing and networking with contacts in the city and afternoons reading and relaxing. Allowing herself the summer off forced Bodie not to jump at the first opportunity that came along—a move that might have landed her in yet another overly stressful and unhappy situation.

"When I first started interviewing in Baltimore, I was offered some very challenging managerial positions that would have paid a salary comparable to what I was making in New York. The jobs sounded exciting but they were extremely demanding.

After the interviews, I would think through the scenario of working Saturdays and late nights and all the travel, and it just didn't feel right. I knew I needed a few years of being on a low burner." At the end of the summer she accepted a job as the number-two public relations person in a small Baltimore advertising agency that handled accounts for local banks and restaurants. "I deliberately took a job where I could ease in and just enjoy myself for a while." But Bodie is not the sort of person who can stay on a low burner for long. Three months after she started the job, her boss left and Bodie was promoted. About six months later her firm merged with a larger Baltimore agency and Bodie was named director of public relations for a firm that had grown overnight from 20 employees to 70.

But even during the busiest periods, Bodie's schedule now is nothing like the 12- to 14-hour days that were the norm for her in New York. "My hours at the moment are about eight to six-thirty and this is as busy as it will ever get." For Bodie, it is the best of both worlds. She has set her own personal limits and come up with an ideal balance: a challenging career that lets her exert her tremendous energy and creativity while allowing her to be near people she loves and feel the sense of community she had longed for in New York. Although she no longer works on the glamour accounts she once did, in a family-oriented city like Baltimore where professional roles are not the dominating force they are in a city like New York, Bodie is a big fish in a relatively small pond. "My family and friends like hearing about what I do. It is still much more exciting than the average job," she says.

Like Vest, Bodie has not given up her ambition but merely found a saner outlet for it. And the sense of continuity and community that comes from knowing her family is only a few miles away allows her to keep her career in better perspective. She now has something else to fall back on. When she has no plans on a Saturday night, her sister, brother- in-law and niece and nephew are a 15-minute drive from her apartment. When she feels like having company while doing her laundry, her parents are ten minutes away. "Just knowing that they are there makes a huge difference. I no longer feel alone in every activity I do. If I have a night when I'm not doing anything, I can always go over and see my family. You always know, no matter what, that you're going to see someone who loves you." Ironically, most of the close friends she has made since moving back home are themselves New York escapees. "I had a few friends here from high school, but I've found the people I have the most in common with had also done their New York stints and can relate to the decision I made."

In another age, what Bodie did would not seem so remarkable. Particularly for single people, there was an assumption 30 years ago that the family one grew up with was still a focal point of one's life. Even when a new family was formed, the grandparents and other members of the extended family were there to help lessen the burden of childcare and ease the way for young parents. But the freedom and mobility implicit in pursuing a career in our society has inevitably meant distancing ourselves physically, as well as emotionally, from the stability and support of family life.

Bodie has been able to achieve that middle ground. While the fast track she had pushed herself along in New York was never really right for her, neither would a highly traditional small-town life have been right. What is most reassuring about the balance Bodie has struck is that it allows her to regain the warmth and closeness of family in a saner living environment without giving up the rewards and sense of accomplishment that come from pursuing a career.

Trading the excitement of a career for the sanity of smalltown life

For Carolyn Bodie, moving to a smaller city meant transferring her ambition to a less visible career track. It did not mean giving up that track completely. Even if the pace has slowed and her professional drive has been tempered by a richer personal life, Bodie's job remains her primary creative and intellectual outlet. For other urban escapees, however, a new system of rewards and career expectations takes over when they make the decision to transplant themselves to a more peaceful physical environment. They intentionally scale back their responsibilities, in many cases either dramatically backtracking or plateauing their careers, as well as their emotional attachment to their work. Some may even admit that their work is a bit dull.

These highly educated and inquisitive professionals may talk about their jobs in a manner more reminiscent of blue-collar workers, who view employment as a means to an end rather than an end in itself. "My job isn't particularly challenging, but it allows me to live the way I want to," admitted Joseph Johnson, who in 1983 transplanted his life and his career from an important management position with the Federal Communications Commission in Washington, D.C., to a rural outpost of the agency in Gettysburg, Pennsylvania, where for six and a half years he headed up computer operations.

One of the most interesting backlashes of the success culture is that it has made boredom suddenly seem appealing. As one Chicago stockbroker put it: "Sometimes I just feel incredibly envious of bus drivers and waiters. They do their jobs and leave them behind. I can never do that." Obviously, there is an element of "the grass is always greener" in such thinking. Unlike the image of the young executive in the Frosted Flakes commercial making his swift retreat to the mailroom in the space of a 30-second ad, the reality of such extreme moves is considerably more tumultuous. The stockbroker, of course, will never give up his six-figure income to drive a bus around Chicago all day. That is the beauty of such fantasies: we know they are just that—fantasies.

But what if the stockbroker were to sit down and seriously consider his alternatives? He might find, as Joseph Johnson did, that he could continue his professional career on a downscaled level that would take him away from the anxieties of his current job and allow him the freedom he associates with a job as a bus driver. He might find that making such a shift would enable him to live in an environment where a six-figure salary would be an absurd extravagance and where there were more hours in the day than he ever imagined to pursue interests and hobbies beyond work. He would also have to accept the idea that although he might be clear in his mind about what he was doing, others would almost certainly question his choice.

When Joseph Johnson told a former boss of his intention to transfer to the low-key Gettysburg office, the top-ranking FCC official's reaction was predictably noncomprehending. "He said, 'You know, if you go up there your career is essentially over. You're never going to go any higher. That's the end of it.'" As Johnson tells it, the former boss then proceeded to pull out his personnel staffing list and offer him every high-level vacancy that he had control over. "He said, 'You take your pick of these jobs.' They were all high-ranking managerial jobs, higher than what I currently had. I thanked him and said I'd think about it, but I never really even gave it another thought."

Joseph Johnson doesn't expect everyone to understand why he gave up an impressive career administering two-way police, taxi and ambulance radio services for the FCC to live in a quiet Pennsylvania town known for a bloody battle fought over a century ago. Although his engineering degree and fascination with radio technology brought him to the FCC in Washington 13 years before, Johnson, who grew up in rural Illinois, had always resisted an urban lifestyle. He commuted to the city virtually the entire time he worked in Washington, and, as the years passed, found himself moving further and further away into the outermost exurbs. By the time he left his Washington job, the divorced Johnson, who had no children at the time, was living 40 miles away in Leesburg, Virginia, and commuting a total of nearly four hours a day to and from work. Still, he never considered living in the city an option. "I have always felt the need to have land and not be scrunched in by lots of people," says Johnson, whose relatively modest government income further limited his options when it came to living closer in.

On the surface, it seemed clear to Johnson that he had to make a choice. His lengthy commute left him little time for a life. But he couldn't imagine simply giving up his highly visible position and promising government career. He also knew his professional options were limited since he had been in government for so many years in managerial rather than technical positions, and that his engineering skills would be considered outdated in private industry. The Gettysburg office of the FCC seemed like a logical alternative—he had visited it a few times on business and was impressed with the operation and people who worked there. Transferring to Gettysburg would also allow him to live in a rural setting while still maintaining his career at the agency, if not moving up in it.

Johnson wrestled with the idea for nearly three years. "I was dating someone at the time, and although it wasn't serious I couldn't see just dropping everything for no obvious reason," recalls Johnson. The reason he needed presented itself when

Johnson was accepted into a master's program he had applied for in electrical engineering at George Washington University, to be paid for by the FCC. It was an opportunity Johnson thought he had wanted for some time, but now he wasn't so sure. Such opportunities, as we have seen with other downshifters, frequently provide the necessary nudge needed to reassess the path one has chosen and clarify what is most important. In Johnson's case, entering the master's program would have meant living in the Washington area for at least another three years. Johnson's reluctance to accept an opportunity he would have jumped at in the past helped him put his priorities into clearer focus. "The more I thought about it, the more I realized that staying in Washington, no matter what the job was, wasn't worth the price of my personal happiness," says Johnson, who is now in his early 40s. He turned down the university program and in the summer of 1983, after making several weekend scouting trips to Gettysburg to check out the town, told his supervisor he wanted to be transferred.

His boss accommodated him with a position as computer systems coordinator for the agency's rural outpost 75 miles from Washington. "Essentially I went from having a career to having a job. I am on no track at all," admits Johnson. But his new life was anything but dull and unchallenging. In fact, with a minimal commute, a less demanding job and a lifestyle so affordable that it turned a $5,000 drop in salary into a net gain of $14,000 annually, Johnson was able to pursue a multitude of interests beyond work, which, he says, made his life feel richer than ever.

Since arriving in Gettysburg in 1984, he has designed and acted as the general contractor of his own 4,000-square-foot Tudor house on 12 acres of rolling farmland outside of Gettysburg. He lives there with his new wife, whom he met through work. He has also subdivided a 100-acre farm and sold off the lots to prospective home builders. "I have been able to channel my creativity into other areas and feel a great sense of accomplishment from projects outside of work that in many ways mean much more to me," says Johnson. His extremely predictable 7 a.m. to 3:30 p.m. work schedule and 10-minute commute through the lush Pennsylvania countryside left Johnson with practically a whole other day after work to pursue outside activities, including talking to people around the world on his extensive ham radio setup and putting the finishing touches on his new home.

Having such interests helped Johnson get through the initial loneliness of relocating to a strange town where there were few social outlets for an unattached male. When Johnson first moved to Gettysburg he was clearly an outsider. "I had no place to go and no one to go with," he admits. During his 13 years in Washington, Johnson had grown accustomed to socializing in a city where transient singles were the norm. The stable, family-oriented world of Gettysburg, by contrast, seemed jarring. For Johnson, however, whose interests had prepared him for rural life, it was just a matter of being patient and establishing his own connections.

For professionals who are more urbanized in their tastes and interests, on the other hand, such transitions to smalltown life may prove quite isolating. Jo-Ann Krestan found the lack of professional notoriety particularly unsettling. "Initially, even though I fought it, my ego really took a beating when I moved out here because I was no longer in a context that valued my achievements," recalls the family therapist and author, who, with her partner Claudia Bepko, transplanted their highly successful suburban New Jersey practice to Brunswick, Maine. Says Krestan: "The first six months I was here, I wanted to stop people on Main Street and say, 'Did you know that I am a very important family therapist?' " Krestan has resolved her need for recognition by visiting old friends and colleagues in New York regularly to "remind myself that my work is highly valued and recognized in certain circles." Being able to return to her more low-key life in Maine, however, allows Krestan to keep a distance from the highly competitive, materialistic culture she has happily left behind.

Although there were adjustments for Johnson as well, what he ultimately came to see was that like everything else in Gettysburg, one's social life simply evolves more slowly—but ultimately more deeply. "The connections here in general are much stronger," says Johnson, who met his new wife after moving to Gettysburg. "There is a feeling of permanence that always seemed to be missing before."

Johnson's story also demonstrates another important facet of downshifting: Making such moves in no ways traps people on a new stifling professional track. In Johnson's case, six and a half years after moving to Gettysburg, the dead-end nature of his job began to eat at him. With his new life established in Gettysburg, he felt it was time to make another shift to a position that offered more challenges. He accepted a job as a senior engineer for the mass media bureau of the FCC, which handles all broadcast regulations. Although the job forces him to make the commute from Gettysburg to Washington, he has worked out a flexible schedule that enables him to beat traffic and make it home before 5 p.m. "My old job allowed me to move to a very pleasant place and have the income to build a great lifestyle, while maintaining my career. Now I feel I can focus again on doing work I find a little more interesting," says Johnson.

To varying degrees Johnson, Vest and Bodie all revised their images of success to encompass a broader and more meaningful form of achievement that valued notions of family and community as much as professional status. Says Bodie: "I have really come to admire my parents for not needing to always have outside stimulation and excitement to lead full lives. They can spend an evening sitting on their porch and just find humor and enjoyment in the simplest things."

In part, for all downshifters, reinventing success also means reconsidering their long-held beliefs about leisure and free time. In this country's smaller cities and towns, there is generally more of an acceptance of the extremely positive value of leisure. For urban professionals, on the other hand, any activity that doesn't produce a tangible reward is frequently viewed as a waste of time. But, as we will see in the next chapter, an appreciation of the type of leisure inherent in smalltown living, no matter where one happens to reside, is crucial if we are to effectively reinvent success, both as individuals and as a society.

8

● ●

Reclaiming the Front Porch

Many of us would hesitate to use the word "leisure" to describe what we do when we are not at work. After all, our prowess on the squash court, our meals at fancy restaurants and our trips to trendy resorts are all part of the professional success package. Rather than leisure, these activities are further proof of our overall accomplishments.

The notion of leisure, in fact, is likely to have negative connotations for those who have steadfastly pursued careers and ever-higher professional goals. A life of excessive leisure is a life that is unserious and unfocused. We equate leisure with idleness, uselessness, even boredom. We may even panic during those rare moments when we have time on our hands. It is as if, in the world beyond the cult of busyness, there lies a lonely abyss, filled with the endless buzz of daytime soap operas and Oprah Winfrey.

While researching this book, I interviewed several people who were openly offended, even distraught, by the idea that professionals should work less. One of them was a corporate headhunter in New York whose attitude reflects a common theme, even among many of those who think about slowing down but can't quite muster the courage. "What you're telling people is that it's all right to be lazy and screw around; to leave the office early so they can have more time to watch tv. Professionals today don't want leisure, they want more work and more responsibility. If they don't have a lot of work and responsibilities, it probably means the ax is about to fall." In those few sentences, the corporate headhunter revealed much about his own fear of free time. Work for many of us is an easy and acceptable way to fill the hours. In our professional lives we have clear rules to follow and goals to meet. By contrast, it is completely up to us to invent the success framework for our leisure. For many of the same reasons, however, that we have been unable to take control of our jobs, we have also found it difficult to take charge of our free time. Instead, whether we are watching television, dining out or attending a sports event, we often end up being passive participants in our leisure lives.

Learning to be successful at free time first means accepting that having enough time after work to pursue activities that are productive and meaningful doesn't imply that we are losers. As we have seen, setting limits in no way means signing your career death sentence. What it does mean is getting used to the idea of having more time for yourself, your family and your community. Like the corporate headhunter, however, many of us recoil at the idea of leisure. Too much of it means we are weak, dull, losers. While we may yearn for the front porch and its promise of community and meaning, we feel it would be an unproductive waste of time to spend an evening or an afternoon sitting on that porch immersed in our thoughts and dreams; talking casually with our neighbors; watching the leaves fall and the sun set.

The loss of leisure

Leisure didn't always have such a bad name. The Greeks believed leisure was the ultimate goal, the essence of freedom. Both Plato and Aristotle saw work as a vehicle for meeting one's basic needs and then moving on to a higher purpose in life—the pursuit of leisure. Plato, in fact, was critical of citizens who kept working after they had met their basic needs. He looked upon Greek career climbers in much the same way we might view the yuppie of the 1980s: He did not feel they were bad, simply misdirected. "They kept on building up wealth, power, reputation, and influence, and being wrapped up in what they mistook as 'important,' 'serious' or 'necessary' work only because they did not know better; having forgotten other more important pursuits," explains Benjamin Hunnicutt in "Plato on Leisure, Play, and Learning." But the price of their ignorance was enormous, points out Hunnicutt: "It was voluntary slavery to incessant 'necessity' and loss of the blessing of leisure; it was work without end."

Thinkers like Plato and Aristotle believed that one of the key functions of education was to teach people "how foolish it was to run from leisure by working too much"; to cover up their fear of freedom by getting caught in the "webs of luxuries, power, politics and excessive amusements." But for the ancient Greeks, the idea of leisure had nothing to do with idleness or laziness, as we think of it today. In Plato's view, leisure was "activity, not passiveness, a mind and body in action, not frozen contemplation." In fact, the Greek word for leisure—"schole"—is the origin of such English words as "school" and "scholar." Learning for the sake of learning—"not for some purpose such as money, product, or obligation"—was the ultimate leisure activity. [1]

Today, of course, when we think of leisure one of the first things that comes to mind is television. It seems fairly clear that watching "Roseanne," "Monday Night Football," and reruns of "Gilligan's Island" was not what the Greeks had in mind when they talked about leisure. The simple fact is, the vast majority of Americans spend the bulk of time when they are not working either sleeping or watching tv. In the past decade alone, according to A.C. Nielsen, television use has risen steadily, from 6 hours and 36 minutes a day per household in 1980 to 7 hours and 2 minutes in 1988. During the past 50 years, idle leisure has become increasingly appealing to Americans, according to Gallup polls taken over several decades. In 1938, the most popular ways to spend an evening were reading, watching movies and dancing. In 1986, the highest honors went to television, followed by resting, relaxing and reading. No one even mentioned resting or relaxing as a favorite leisure-time activity in the 1938 survey.

With our exhausting careers to contend with, the last thing we want is to be intellectually or creatively challenged during our leisure time. As a result, the less involving and thought-provoking the activity, the more attractive it is. Who wants to sit down and play a heady game of chess after a day of endless meetings and incessant demands? We want mindlessness, and marketers are more than willing to lend us a hand. The inventor of one of the most popular adult board games of the late eighties, Adverteasing, which tests players' ability to identify advertising jingles, admits that the game's primary appeal is that it doesn't force people to think. "You can be totally uneducated and play Adverteasing," boasts Richard Levy, the game's creator. "We live in an age of 30-second television commercials. With Adverteasing, you can open the box and you know how to play." [2]

One reason for the growing emphasis on idle, thoughtless leisure activities is that what might once have been considered more worthwhile leisure pursuits have now taken the form of obligation. The "gotta run, I'll call you, we'll do lunch" phenomenon is a prime example of this. The uncomplicated pleasure of sharing a meal with a good friend has become one more activity to be scheduled in during the rushed, overburdened workday. Even such natural leisure activities as conversation and sex are now penciled in on pocket calendars. I have a friend who is so pressed for time that she schedules personal phone calls to friends—down to the specific time and day that the conversation will take place. One man I spoke with, a therapist who counsels time-hungry fast-trackers, actually schedules in a half-hour of intimacy or what he calls "pillow-talk" each morning with his own wife. "We both know that if we don't make a point of doing it, with our busy schedules, we may forget," he says.

This type of scheduled leisure has played well in an age of high-tech efficiency when our success so often seems to be measured by how many activities we can cram into a day. Leisure is just one more rushed, overscheduled obligation, often performed while we are doing something else. We read the newspaper while riding our exercise bike; we hold a meeting over our car phone while wolfing down a take-out sandwich. One fan of Adverteasing says she likes the game because it allows her to do other things, such as making dinner and washing the dishes, while playing. "It's not like playing chess where you have to be seated all the time and make a move every few minutes."[3]

In a parody of our overscheduled modern lives, *USA Today* calculated that we would need 42 hours to accomplish everything in a given day that the experts say is required of the well-rounded, healthy, balanced individual of the 1990s. This includes 30 minutes for exercise, 45 minutes for personal grooming, 2 to 4 hours with the children and spouse (according to pediatricians and psychologists), 45 minutes to read the newspapers, 1.5 hours commuting (a "realistic" average for most suburban commuters, according to The Conference Board), 7 to 10 hours working, 1 to 2 hours on housekeeping and chores, 50 minutes for sex and intimacy, plus another 15 minutes here or an hour there for such activities as cooking and eating dinner, taking care of the plants, reading a book, listening to music and sleeping. [4]

Sleep, of course, has become the big proving ground. The less of it we can get by on, the more dynamic, successful and basically superior we are. I used to be embarrassed myself to admit that I needed eight hours of sleep a night to feel my best. Everyone around me seemed to be getting by on no more than six and a half—or at least that's what they claimed. When a story appeared in the *New York Times* in May 1990 suggesting that most experts feel the average person needs seven to nine hours of sleep a night, I felt vindicated. [5] I wasn't a low-energy loser after all.

Increasingly, our leisure activities seem to embody many of the characteristics of work. The way we use our leisure time, in this sense, becomes another form of competition, another means of standing out from the crowd. This growing link between work and leisure actually has developed during the past century as Americans have come to view leisure as something that only money can buy. Like the homes on Newark Street with their beautiful empty porches, leisure was something one had, not something one did. Luxury and entertainment became synonymous with leisure.

Historically, this changing definition of leisure is tied to a gradual shift in the American definition of progress from dreams of more leisure and a shorter work week to an obsession with work and material advancement as the ticket to personal and spiritual fulfillment. In his book *Work Without End,* Benjamin Hunnicutt points out that during the hundred years prior to the Depression, social reformers, labor, community and religious leaders and progressive politicians worked to reduce the work week, believing that having more time for family, hobbies and civic participation was the greatest measure of success in industrial society. Intellectuals promoted shorter hours as "an alternative to work, as an avenue for human progress, leading the common man to exercise his higher faculties—mind, body and spirit—in a democratic culture."[6]

The more leisure time we had the greater our progress as a society. That meant working less, not more. After years of struggle against resistant employers, in the late 1930s the fight for freedom from work resulted in the national standard of the 40-hour, five-day work week. The quest for further reductions was mounted during the next few years, as labor and congressional leaders and even members of the Roosevelt administration fought for a 30-hour work week. But continued employer resistance, combined with a growing negative perception of leisure following the massive unemployment of the Depression, all but halted the shorter-hour movement. More jobs for more people became the answer to the country's economic troubles. Work became the great savior.[7]

The notion of work and free time during this same period—about 1920 to 1940—underwent a dramatic shift as Madison Avenue began selling a new form of leisure, one that by its very nature encouraged material gain. American manufacturers had just begun to produce a variety of leisure goods and services. But they needed people to buy those products. If Americans started working shorter hours and had less discretionary income, the result could be a "crisis of overproduction." Thus was born the gospel of conspicuous consumption. With the help of the emerging advertising industry, Americans were urged to consume more leisure items and services. This new economic gospel of consumption endorsed the idea of leisure as long as it led people to buy more things: to "spend" their leisure. Henry Ford called leisure "a cold business fact," necessary for promoting such new industries as hotels, radio, phonographs, motion pictures, amusements and publishing.[8]

Advertisers during this period even began to suggest that time not spent working or consuming was unpatriotic, and planted the idea of "socially motivated consumption." Business leaders helped the cause by continuing their defense against shorter hours by promoting work, not leisure, as the greatest place for individual self-expression and cultural progress. Work was "a joy," a "wonder," "the American secret," "the developer of character," an "adventure" and a source of "spiritual inspiration." Progress, for the first time, was now defined as "new jobs, new products and an ever higher standard of living," rather than as a "resolution of the economic problem in favor of the satisfactions of the mind and spirit."[9]

All of this led neatly into the upwardly mobile post–World War II period, when the dream of home ownership and weekends on the golf course further fueled the notion that more work was necessary in order to achieve the good life. This was also the beginning of the human resources movement in industry. The workplace was now being touted as a collegial, empathetic family where "the organization man" could live out his working years in security and comfort. Managers in the 1950s were urged to "get to know" their employees, to "relate to them" as human beings. Companies demonstrated their devotion to the individual by sponsoring bowling teams, company picnics and fairs.[10]

Much of our current leisure imagery was created during the 1950s. Despite the decade's reputation for complacency, it was a period, as we have seen, that had a powerful effect on the way many professionals today map out their own lives. Leisure in the 1950s came to represent everything that was uninspired and unoriginal about suburban middle-class culture. Leisure was golf on the weekends and male conformity; it was volunteering at the local church and female oppression. The powerful effect of these images caused many of today's professionals to run as far away from their roots—both emotionally and geographically—as their minds and bodies would take them. In their mad dash to be different, however, they left behind many of the things that mattered most. Behind the stereotypical 1950s imagery was a devotion to family, community and simple pleasures that have been almost entirely absent from the busy lives of many of today's career climbers.

Work, instead, has been our salvation. The corporate human potential movement, which was initiated in 1960 with the publication of Douglas McGregor's *The Human Side of Enterprise,* ignited our belief that work is supposed to be the most satisfying and worthwhile of all pursuits. "Meaningful work," promised management pundits, would automatically translate into a "meaningful life." This theme was carried through into the 1970s, although the emphasis shifted slightly to notions of creativity and "self-actualization." T-groups and executive encounter sessions replaced bowling parties and company picnics. In the 1980s, the principles of "excellence," "quality" and "customer satisfaction" dominated the writings of management theorists and continued to send a message to employees that the work they were doing "made a difference." Throughout all of this, the emerging service sector, with its emphasis on "working with people" and doing "work that mattered," provided the ideal breeding ground for new-age management theories.

In such a professional world, a concern with leisure seemed frivolous and unnecessary. What could be more satisfying, after all, than being a member of a community that shared a common sense of mission and purpose, which strove to make both its employees and customers live fuller and happier lives and which viewed work as an outlet for creative and personal expression? In fact, the view of work during the postwar era has increasingly taken on the characteristics of what psychologists typically define as leisure activities. In a 1986 study, Howard E.A. Tinsley and Diane J. Tinsley, professors of psychology at Southern Illinois University, found that individuals experiencing "leisure" feel the following:

1. Total absorption in (or intense concentration on) the activity at hand.
2. Lack of focus on (or forgetting of) self.
3. Feelings of freedom.
4. Enriched perception of objects and events.
5. Increased sensitivity to bodily sensations.
6. Increased sensitivity to and intensity of emotions.
7. Decreased awareness of the passage of time.

These and similar feelings have been described by some psychologists as the state of "optimal experience" or *flow*. According to University of Chicago psychologist Mihaly Csikszentmihalyi, those experiencing *flow* feel "a sense of participation in determining the content of life that comes as close to what is usually meant by happiness as anything else we can conceivably imagine."[11]

Many of us may experience some or even most of these feelings while working on a project we feel especially committed to or inspired by. For the most part, however, the reason so many professionals are frustrated with their careers today is that the bottom-line realities of most jobs can never fulfill these exaggerated expectations. Rather than putting all our energies into our jobs, we need instead to learn to appreciate and excel in our leisure activities as well. We need to discover that true satisfaction comes from leading a meaningful life, not simply doing meaningful work.

Revising our leisure imagery first means getting used to

the idea of freedom. As we have seen throughout this book, a sense of freedom is remarkably absent from the controlled, over-scheduled lives of most career climbers. If one works 60 hours a week and spends the rest of the time doing errands, sleeping and trying to relax, freedom can start to seem like an empty concept. Getting used to freedom—to the feeling of not being so tired at the end of the day that the only thing you have the energy for is television—is the most challenging and rewarding aspect of downshifting. Slowing down their careers has enabled the people in this book to tap into areas of their lives that many had ignored for years. In changing their concept of success, they have also reinvented their long-held notions about leisure.

Time for yourself

The first few months after cutting back are often the most difficult for downshifters. Many experience feelings of panic. Suddenly all those hours that used to be taken up by work and responsibility are now open to them to fill in any way they see fit. For many it is a frightening, even unnatural feeling.

Jo-Ann Krestan's experience was typical. When she first transplanted her career as a writer and family therapist to a quiet Maine town, for the first time in years she found herself with time on her hands. In her book, *Too Good for Her Own Good: Breaking Free from the Burden of Female Responsibility,* written with partner Claudia Bepko, Krestan describes the feelings of joy followed by guilt and then panic that took hold one day when she began engaging in activities that were only for her:

> I decided to go to the nearby college library to get myself a library card—something I had not had time to do in the past twenty years of working

hard at my career. Seduced by the stacks, and taken back in time thirty years to my enjoyable days in college when I often went to the library for the pure pleasure of exploring books and ideas, I picked up a journal that had no relevance whatever to some work that I had been doing on a new topic for a speech. I read an article on a famous woman writer. I leafed through an anthropology book. I imagined myself being an undergraduate student again and felt flooded with joy. I was doing nothing much, certainly not working, and suddenly I was having all kinds of pleasurable feelings and fantasies. I was enjoying myself.

Then I thought that I should really get home. I started to feel very anxious. The dog was in the car—maybe she was cold. Probably, I told myself, I could xerox the articles and read them later. I made myself sit there, aware of the inner dialogue between my two voices—the voice that knew my rising overresponsibility didn't even have a focus or an object and was ridiculous, and the voice that told me I was something "bad" for enjoying myself and wasting time with no redeeming purpose. Having chosen to do nothing of importance, I was beginning to feel things that were confusing. I was facing an unfamiliar impulse in myself.

By now, my enjoyment was disrupted. I was back in my trance of responsibility, so I put my articles away and went home. The dog was fine and didn't say a word. Neither did any of the people at home. Nobody had really needed my attention but myself. Maybe that's what was so disconcerting. [12]

Crossing over the void that lies between the cult of busyness and overresponsibility and the freedom and pure joy that comes from having time for ourselves can be one of the most satisfying results of downshifting. Most of us, however, have come to rely on our professional responsibilities to fill in the empty spaces and define who we are. As a result, participating in activities that are purely for ourselves, as Krestan found, may at first feel unsettling. Some downshifters initially respond to these feelings by actually trying to create more work for themselves. Back-tracker Ray Everngam, who left his high-pressure position with the National Association of Social Workers for a lower-key publishing job, continued to conduct his life according to the rhythms of an all-consuming job, even though it was no longer necessary. He would venture to the office on weekends just because it was what he was used to doing and wolf down lunch in 15 minutes so that he could get back to his desk before missing an important phone call.

By allowing themselves to live through those feelings of guilt and panic, downshifters like Everngam and Krestan ultimately learn that it is all right to pursue interests and get involved in activities that are rewarding for no other reason than that they bring them joy and satisfaction. Sadly, many career climbers become so accustomed to focusing all or most of their intellectual and emotional energies on narrow career goals that they forget what it feels like to pursue an interest that is only for them. Most highly successful professionals, in fact, have typically been rewarded for their career tunnel vision—not their broad and eclectic interests. As a result, excavating those often deeply buried passions will require rediscovering old dreams and fantasies and perhaps coming up with a new set of life goals.

Many may even be embarrassed to admit they have outside interests beyond those typically engaged in by their community of professional friends and colleagues, such as working out at the health club, going out to dinner, seeing an occasional movie or play. Not that there is anything wrong with such leisure pursuits—I participate in all of them myself on a regular basis. In most cases, however, these "professional leisure activities" stop short of allowing us to tap into the passions and talents that make us special. In her book *Wishcraft,* Barbara Sher writes that we are all "Renaissance people—that a single human brain contains many more capacities than we realize." As evidence she points to the whimsical and exuberant answers her subjects gave when asked the simple question, "What might you have been?" Said one: "I'd have published a novel, and I'd play folk guitar, and I'd be studying mime, sign language, drums, Spanish and Japanese." Responded another: "I'd be the originator and head of a very unusual kind of textile center—a design and manufacturing center for fabrics and a learning institution. Or I'd be a painter. Or an anthropologist. And a folksinger in 20 languages on the side." [13]

The point is not necessarily to *become* all those things but to start allowing ourselves to tap into our long-dormant childhood fantasies. One part of me still holds onto a childhood dream of becoming an actress. Downshifting, in my case, would provide the perfect opportunity to explore those interests in a real-life context, perhaps by signing up for drama classes or even auditioning with a community theater group.

Thinking this way allows us to start setting new goals for ourselves that will make our leisure life, as well as our professional life, richer and more satisfying. Ray Everngam's fantasy was to be a writer. "I always wanted to write the Great American Novel. But I had convinced myself that it was a silly and frivolous goal because it would never advance me professionally. For a long time, anything that didn't get me ahead in my career I shoved out of my life." With his new, predictable schedule, which brought him home by 4:30 or 5 every evening, Everngam now had the time and inclination to "just write for the fun of it, whether or not it got me anywhere." Everngam overcame the initial period of panic and the feelings that he should be "doing something productive" by setting himself on a fairly rigid writing schedule. He now spends two or three evenings a week and all day Saturday writing a novel that he knows may never get published. "Writing for me now is just a relaxing activity. It's like creating my own entertainment, my own videotapes in my head."

Writing has also helped Everngam tap into parts of himself that had been buried during his years of chasing professional rewards. "I am learning about a whole aspect of myself that I didn't realize was there before. It is the part of me that isn't so competitive and consumed by the workaday world." The exploration and development of characters in the book has also proven an important cathartic exercise for Everngam. "The book is the story of a father and son who are going on a journey of self-discovery. The setting for the journey is a hike in the Grand Canyon on an oppressively hot day and each learns a lot about himself and the other as he makes the trip. There are definitely elements of myself in the son. A big part of it is my relationships with other people, the feeling of being connected and being part of something larger than my career. Working it out through the development of the son's character has helped me come to terms with what is most important in my own life."

Like Everngam, many downshifters realize, often for the first time in their adult lives, that they really do have the freedom to create or build virtually anything they want. They discover new outlets for self-expression that are often more exciting and rewarding than all their past professional accomplishments put together. Joseph Johnson's dream was to build his own house.

For years he had carried around a vision of what he wanted. When he left his job with the FCC in Washington, D.C., to move to the rural Gettysburg outpost, he realized that the cheap cost of land and construction meant he would now have the chance to live out his fantasy.

For two or three months, Johnson spent several hours after work drawing up the plans, something he had plenty of time for with his new schedule. His first step was to build a garage with an apartment over it, where he could oversee the construction of the home. He lived there for two years while the house was being constructed, every day watching a piece of his dream go up before his eyes. He not only drew up the plans and acted as general contractor but did much of the physical work, including putting up the insulation, hauling material, building walls and installing doors. "When the house was in move-in condition, I sawed the wall myself connecting the apartment to the house and walked through the passage. It was an incredible feeling," says Johnson.

For several months afterward, Johnson continued to put the finishing touches on the house when he got home from work in the evening, including turning the attic into an enormous master bedroom. But the sense of pure accomplishment Johnson has felt from completing each new task is hard to match anywhere else in his life. "The feeling I have every day when I wake up in a house that is *mine* in every sense of the word is much deeper than any amount of job satisfaction. There is nothing quite like it."

Leisure goals, of course, don't have to be as big as building a house or as lofty as writing a novel. Downshifters, for instance, not only have more time to see plays, visit museums, participate in a favorite sport and take more vacations; they also have both the time and inclination to truly enjoy and appreciate such activities. That is not always easy when such activities are wedged into rushed workdays. When my soon-to-be-husband and I, for example, decided to get season tickets for a local theater group, we thought it would be a good way to force ourselves to start taking advantage of the city's multiple cultural offerings. But between deadlines for work and this book, I often found myself resenting the fact that I had to spend an evening at the theater, and at least half the time could not completely appreciate the plays I was seeing—even though under more relaxed circumstances I would have enjoyed them immensely.

Part of the problem is a lack of space between work and leisure. Leaving the office at 7:30 p.m. to catch an 8 p.m. performance didn't allow me enough time to shift gears and focus on the new activity. Instead my mind reeled with concerns over how I would organize a particular article or who I could interview the next day for that quote I needed. In a similar way, other "efficient" forms of leisure, such as tacking pleasure travel onto business trips, often defeat the purpose of undertaking the activity in the first place. The joy, for instance, that comes from choosing a vacation destination, planning a trip and then immersing ourselves in a new culture or experience can rarely be achieved when one suitcase is packed with business clothes and notes from yesterday's client presentation and the other with swimsuits and trashy novels.

Nowhere has this problem of overefficient leisure been more evident in recent years than in our athletic pursuits. During the past decade, the fitness craze turned the notion of relaxed, noncompetitive sports into another pressured, goal-oriented activity. Not only were we urged to join health clubs to stay more youthful and keep our bodies in shape, but we were told that working out would make us more productive on the job and give us more energy to work ever-longer hours. Many of us obediently followed these marching orders. By 1989, 16.6 million people belonged to health clubs, according to the Association of

Fitness Professionals. Getting in our 45 minutes of pumping, running and stretching became one more requirement on the road to the executive suite.

Ironically, the very physical activities that are supposed to help us relieve stress can actually end up putting on more pressure as we rush to get to the aerobics class on time or quickly wind up our early-morning jog in order to make it to the office by 8 a.m. Self-employer Diane Davis Reed found it impossible to fully benefit from the physical activities she enjoyed most—walking, jogging, meditation and the Oriental martial art of tai chi—during her highly structured and demanding years as a corporate human resources manager. As Reed says, "It doesn't work well to feel rushed and meditate." Her new, slower-track arrangement as an affiliate to a career counseling firm has allowed her to establish a more leisurely morning routine.

For two hours each morning, Reed completely absorbs herself in a ritual consisting of a two-mile walk or jog, meditation and tai chi, which focuses on balance and relaxation. For Reed, these activities are as important to achieving a balance in her life as having a reasonable work schedule. "It is a physical expression of balance that translates into the rest of my life. When I don't have time to do these things the rest of my life starts feeling out of whack." No longer burdened by a rigid corporate schedule, Reed is now able to run that extra half-mile, just because she is in the mood or because it is a particularly beautiful day. Exercise has become a joy rather than a chore. On one radiant spring morning she noticed, for the first time, the sweet smell of the Russian olive tree. "I ran past this row of trees and couldn't believe how fragrant they were. I ran back and went in circles several times just to keep smelling them." When Reed mentioned the incident to her mother, it provoked an emotional response she could never have anticipated. "She said it was one of her favorite smells from childhood and for the first time I was connecting with it too. I couldn't believe I had never even noticed that they had a fragrance."

What downshifters like Reed come to discover is that there is no such thing as quality time when your job consumes so much of your life that the hours away from work are spent trying to either squeeze in "leisure" activities or simply recuperate from another hectic day. Full appreciation and involvement in an activity, whether you are jogging through your neighborhood, writing fiction or helping your daughter master her two-wheeler, is what true quality leisure time is all about.

Time for family

One of the problems with the so-called quality time argument when it comes to balancing demanding work schedules with childcare is that like most forms of scheduled leisure, the time actually spent with the kids ends up being so weighted down by obligation that it feels more like work than play. "I always felt like I was being pulled in so many directions that I couldn't feel good about anything I was doing—whether I was working or going to the zoo with my children," recalls self-employer Valerie Fisher of her years spent trying to work part-time for a large Chicago law firm.

This, of course, is one reason why some professional women, and even a few men, are opting to give up their careers entirely for several years to stay home with their children. The ability to place limits on their careers and gain control of their lives helps downshifters achieve a middle-ground alternative that many say allows them to keep both their career and family lives in better balance. Rather than being distinctly separate chunks of their lives, work and family start to naturally flow together.

Sociologists have noted that the separate paths to achievement laid out in schools and professions, on one hand, and by family and personal obligations, on the other, have been especially powerful in shaping our success roles in modern society. Rather than being intertwined as part of daily life, as these functions were on, say, the idealized nineteenth-century family farm, they now often seem to be battling each other for space in our cluttered lives.

Often for the first time, downshifters discover that family and work life can be integrated in a way that makes both more enjoyable. Those who experience this most vividly are professionals who work at home at least part of the time. Self-employer and financial analyst Matthew Lind cherishes the two days a week he spends running up data on his home computer. "My activities naturally seem to mesh together. I can take periodic breaks to spend time with my kids and just be there when they need me around. I feel like I'm much more a part of their life."

Without exception, all of the downshifters with young children interviewed for this book said the time spent with their families had stopped seeming like obligation or work and had started to feel more like true leisure. "When I was home in the past, I was a perfect shit, to put it bluntly," says Lind, whose relationship with his wife and young daughter suffered under the pressure of his long hours and stressful commute. "All I wanted was peace and quiet and to be left alone. Even when my daughter Kate was a baby and would wake up crying in the middle of the night, my only concern was that she quiet down so I could sleep. There was absolutely no empathy for either her or my wife, who would always be the one to get up." With his new, slower-track schedule and attitude, Lind is now often the first to jump out of bed and comfort his infant son Sam when he wakes at night. The time he spends with his daughter is no longer burdened by the anxieties of the office. "When I'm working at home Kate and I will often head to the grocery store together or go out to lunch, and it feels completely relaxed and natural. We're getting to know each other."

Former NBC News correspondent Ken Bode had always worked hard to make time for his family and be an involved parent. But, as he readily admits, when you are hardly ever home that involvement can only go so far. "What was really missing before was the ability to spend mundane time together," recalls Bode. It's the little things, Bode has found, that create an overall sense of belonging to a close and connected family. It is responding to a daughter's complaints of feeling bored on a Saturday afternoon by jumping in the car with her and driving to the nearest antique shops in search of that perfect old cabinet. It is bringing the rickety furniture back home, showing his daughter how to strip the paint and refinish it, and then watching with pride as she absorbs herself in her new project.

For Bode and his family, quality leisure time is a mix of uncomplicated routine and lighthearted spontaneity. "The other night after dinner we all got up and played a game of volleyball and then jumped in the pool. Those things just happen now. They are part of everyday life. My daughter Matilda will do things like call me up at the office and ask if she can come over to study. She'll then show up with three or four friends and take over the little conference room because it's more fun than being in the library. It's the intangibles like that, nothing remarkable, that make the biggest difference."

Time for community

When downshifters step back from their cocoonlike careers, as we have seen, remarkable things begin to happen: They start to focus more on their true interests and needs; they form deeper connections to family and close friends, and many begin to see that becoming involved in the larger community is far more satisfying than restricting their focus to the community of work.

In retrospect, the emphasis on extreme self-reliance and individualism that characterized the 1980s now seems somewhat ludicrous. The depressing facts of a decade of noninvolvement were revealed in a 1989 poll of young Americans, aged 15 to 24, conducted for the group People for the American Way. When asked to pick the goals that were most important to them, 72 percent of those surveyed chose "being successful in a job or career" compared with 24 percent who picked "being involved in helping the community to be a better place." Three out of five were not involved in any form of community service, and only one-third said they could foresee a time when they might join the military or work as a volunteer in a political campaign. They typically blamed the demands of their personal life for precluding involvement in civic activities. Fifty-three percent said the pressures of "getting good grades or getting a good job" were the main reasons for their lack of involvement.

Such attitudes, of course, do not evolve in a vacuum. Eighty-four percent of social studies teachers interviewed for the study cited a lack of parental encouragement as the primary reason for student apathy. As one teacher said: "If parents don't have time to deal with the Girl Scouts or the heart campaign or politicking in the community or cleaning up their neighborhood, the kids won't."

The whole notion of achievement in our society inherently leads to isolation from the larger community. Our real goal, in fact, is to rise high enough above that community to be able to look down on those who haven't made it. "The American dream," writes sociologist Robert N. Bellah and his colleagues in *Habits of the Heart*, "is often a very private dream of being the star, the uniquely successful and admirable one, the one who stands out from the crowd of ordinary folks who don't know how." What we have lost in this modern privatization of the American Dream is our sense of citizenship. Notes Bellah: "We have put our own good, as individuals, as groups, as a nation, ahead of the common good." [14] Our success is not judged by how much we contribute, but how much we manage to take.

The lack of a strong, institutionalized support system for volunteerism in American society further fuels the emphasis on career over cause. In our culture, writes Bellah, "the rules of the competitive market, not the practices of the town meeting or the fellowship of the church, are the real arbiters of living." [15] Striking a balance between "the kind of self-interest implicit in the individualistic search for success and the kind of concern required to gain the joys of community and public involvement" [16] means learning to feel successful even if personal triumphs are overshadowed by the larger mission.

Many of the downshifters I spoke with continued to express a concern that they weren't "contributing enough." Some even chastised themselves for not being as active in their communities as they had hoped to be after slowing down their careers. "I guess I'm a little disappointed in myself," confessed urban escapee Carolyn Bodie. "I had hoped to make my community activities almost like a second job. But it just isn't realistic." When pressed, however, Bodie conceded that she was perhaps more involved than she gave herself credit for. She was on the board of a nonprofit art gallery devoted to promoting the careers of local artists and was co-chairperson for the gallery's summer gala. She also had done career counseling for girls at her old high school and, through her public relations job for a local ad agency, was working on several pro bono campaigns, including a publicity effort for a child abuse prevention center in Baltimore.

Bodie's feelings of "not doing enough" are typical of successful professionals who are used to throwing themselves completely into whatever activity they are pursuing. For Bodie, if her volunteer work didn't represent the equivalent of a "second job" it meant she wasn't truly committed. After achieving at such a high professional level, Bodie didn't feel it was enough to be a relatively minor participant in a larger cause.

Many professional women like Bodie are especially leery of falling into the docile volunteer role they associate with the 1950s housewife. While their mothers seemed content to volunteer at the local church or school, and stuff envelopes for their favorite local politician, these women want to play either a dramatically different role or none at all. Recalls back-tracker Wendy Osborn Stenzel, who ultimately cut back her job at Tandem to have more time to work against nuclear proliferation: "I grew up having disdain for the stay-at-home mother and volunteer. But I was starting to realize that I knew nothing about what those women really did."

Downshifters like Stenzel begin to see the value of simply playing a part—no matter how small. For some this may start by taking a more active role in their church or synagogue. Says management consultant Carolyn McCormick: "My husband and I recently started going to church again because we both felt a spiritual absence in our lives. It gives us a base, a sense of community and being part of something larger than our narrow professional worlds." Like McCormick, a growing number of professionals are seeking a more active involvement in their religious communities. In the last half of the 1980s, 43 percent of baby boomers attended church or synagogue on a regular basis (three times a month or more), according to David Roozen, director of the Hartford Seminary Center for Social and Religious Research. He expects that number to continue to grow in the next decade as more baby boomer-aged professionals move into parenting roles and search for "deeper and more meaningful lives."

By putting limits on their careers, downshifters also open up opportunities to connect to the larger community through the work they do. For some, like Carolyn Bodie, that means having the time and opportunity to offer their services on a pro bono basis. By not pursing an equity-holding partnership position at his Boston law firm, plateauer Stuart Rossman was also able to devote more time to community work, including chairing the firm's pro bono committee. For other downshifters, connecting to the community often comes down to doing work they feel is more inherently meaningful. By plateauing his career at Du Pont and turning down promotions into the corporate suite, Mark Deschere has been able to make lateral moves into assignments that "allow me to contribute more directly to the society as a whole." As we saw, Deschere has most recently worked on the company's Freon alternatives program.

In many cases, meaningful work means simply sticking to principles and not sacrificing what these professionals know to be good, honest quality work. For Oak Park, Illinois, lawyers Valerie Fisher, Robin Schirmer and Cheryl Berdelle, it means refusing to rubber-stamp such transactions as real-estate closings. "A lot of small legal offices and sole proprietors get into the business of churning out five house closings a day. They make a mint at it, but there is very little thought or care put into what they are doing," says Schirmer. "For us, it just wouldn't be worth it to operate like that. Perhaps somewhat naïvely, we spend time and effort on each closing and usually end up doing no more than ten or twelve a month. We don't make as much money, but at least we can feel we are offering our clients quality service."

As Schirmer and her partners have come to recognize, reinventing success often comes down to accepting less, and realizing that by doing so, we actually gain more. Downshifters internalize the notion of setting limits as a part of their revised success imagery. With this new imagery to guide them, they are far less tempted to sacrifice good and meaningful work for greater material or external professional rewards.

Downshifters are no longer impressed by the splashy Hollywood success imagery. Instead, the new pictures in their heads are more eloquent, thoughtful and, ultimately, more satisfying. The front porch may not be as grand or the house it is attached to as large. But in this new picture, they are sitting on that porch, chatting with the neighbors, writting a letter to a friend and rereading that favorite old classic.

Accepting our limits

More than a century ago, John Stuart Mill predicted that if the Western world continued along the ever-expanding path we have in fact taken, we would destroy the environment: "The earth must lose that great portion of its pleasantness which it owes to things that the unlimited increase in wealth . . . would extirpate from it. . . . I sincerely hope, for the sake of posterity, that [future generations] will be content to be stationary, long before necessity compels them to it." [17] In a world of limited resources, the idea of limitlessness is, of course, impossible. The environment, as we are now clearly seeing, cannot stand up to the demands placed on it by an energy-hungry modern culture.

As individuals and as a society we need to reinvent our notion of progress. John F. Kennedy believed there were no limits to what America could achieve, and most of us have interpreted that to mean there were no limits to how high we could climb or how much we could have. But perhaps it is time for a new interpretation that focuses on our unlimited capacity as human beings to adapt and change; to, in fact, accept our limits and recognize that within those boundaries the possibilities for leading fuller lives are, well, limitless.

Notes

Chapter 1

1. Michael Korda, *Success!* (New York: Ballantine, 1978), p. 4.
2. Barbara Ehrenreich, *Fear of Falling: The Inner Life of the Middle Class* (New York: Pantheon, 1989).
3. *Ibid.,* p. 12.
4. Letter to the Editor, *Working Woman* (March 1989), p. 42.
5. Herbert A. Shepard, "On the Realization of Human Potential: A Path with Heart," *Working with Career* (New York: Columbia University School of Business, 1984), p. 30.

Chapter 2

1. Sally Solo, "Stop Whining and Get Back to Work," *Fortune* (March 12, 1990), pp. 49–50.
2. James M. McPherson, *Battle Cry of Freedom* (New York: Ballantine, 1989), p. 6.
3. *Ibid.,* pp. 6–7.
4. Jeremy Rifkin, *Time Wars* (New York: Simon & Schuster, 1987), pp. 123–124.
5. *Ibid.,* pp. 124–128.
6. *Ibid.,* pp. 138–141.
7. Ehrenreich, *Fear of Falling,* p. 199.
8. Douglas McGregor, *The Human Side of Enterprise* (New York: McGraw-Hill, 1960).
9. Robert Townsend, *Up the Organization* (New York: Alfred A. Knopf, 1970), p. 142.

Notes

· · · · · ·

10. Donald L. Kanter and Philip H. Mirvis, *The Cynical Americans* (San Francisco, CA: Jossey-Bass, 1989), p. 124.

11. Michael Maccoby, *The Gamesman* (New York: Simon & Schuster, 1976).

12. Kanter and Mirvis, *The Cynical Americans*.

13. *Ibid.,* p. 144.

14. Maccoby, *The Gamesman*.

15. Douglas LaBier, *Modern Madness: The Emotional Fallout of Success* (Reading, MA: Addison-Wesley, 1986), pp. 54–56.

Chapter 3

1. Allen H. Neuharth, *Confessions of an S.O.B.* (New York: Doubleday, 1989).

2. Judith M. Bardwick, *The Plateauing Trap* (New York: Bantam, 1988), pp. 47–48.

3. *Ibid.,* pp. 48–49.

4. *Ibid.,* p. 55.

5. Neuharth, *Confessions of an S.O.B.*

6. Peter T. Kilborn, "Companies That Temper Ambition," *New York Times* (February 27, 1990).

Chapter 4

1. Tracy Kidder, *The Soul of a New Machine* (New York: Avon, 1981), p. 66.

2. Kanter and Mirvis, *The Cynical Americans,* p. 128.

Chapter 5

1. Rebecca Voelker, "Women MDs Lead Way to Work Flexibility," *American Medical News* (May 5, 1989), pp. 15, 19.

Chapter 6

1. Rosabeth Moss Kanter, *When Giants Learn to Dance* (New York: Simon & Schuster, 1989), p. 316.

2. Denie S. Weil, "Doing Business in the 'Burbs,' " *Working Woman* (August 1989), p. 58.

3. Eve Broudy, *Professional Temping* (New York: Collier, 1989), p. 11.

Chapter 7

1. Henry David Thoreau, "Walden," in *The Writings of Henry David Thoreau* (Boston, MA: Houghton Mifflin, 1906).

2. David E. Shi, *In Search of the Simple Life* (Layton, UT: Peregrine Smith, 1986), p. 229.

3. *Ibid.,* p. 280.

4. Interview with Patty Feld, 1989.

5. Robert Levine, with Ellen Wolf, "Social Time: The Heartbeat of Culture," *Psychology Today* (March 1985).

6. Daniel Yankelovich, "New Rules in American Life: Searching for Self-

Notes

......

Fulfillment in a World Turned Upside Down," *Psychology Today* (April 1981), p. 74.

Chapter 8

1. Benjamin Kline Hunnicutt, "Plato on Leisure, Play and Learning," *Leisure Sciences* (Summer 1990).
2. Lena Williams, "Adults Play Hard at Nongame Games," *New York Times,* (October 18, 1988).
3. *Ibid., New York Times.*
4. Karen S. Peterson, "There's No Way to Beat the Clock," *USA Today* (April 13, 1989).
5. Natalie Angier, "Cheating on Sleep: Modern Life Turns America into the Land of the Drowsy," *New York Times* (May 15, 1990).
6. Benjamin Kline Hunnicutt, *Work Without End: Abandoning Shorter Hours for the Right to Work* (Philadelphia, PA: Temple University Press, 1988), p. 2.
7. *Ibid.,* p. 45.
8. *Ibid.,* p. 47.
9. *Ibid.,* p. 65.
10. Kanter and Mirvis, *The Cynical Americans.*
11. Mihaly Csikszentmihalyi, *Flow: The Psychology of Optimal Experience* (New York: Harper & Row, 1990), p. 4.
12. Claudia Bepko and Jo-Ann Krestan, *Too Good for Her Own Good: Breaking Free from the Burden of Female Responsibility* (New York: Harper & Row, 1990), p. 154.
13. Barbara Sher, with Annie Gottlieb, *Wishcraft: How to Get What You Really Want* (New York: Ballantine, 1979), p. 26.
14. Robert N. Bellah, Richard Madsen, William M. Sullivan, Ann Swindler, and Steven M. Tipton, *Habits of the Heart* (New York: Harper & Row, 1985), p. 235.
15. *Ibid.,* p. 251.
16. *Ibid.,* p. 199.
17. Quoted in Benjamin Hunnicutt, "No Time for God or Family," *Wall Street Journal* (January 4, 1990).

Index

231

Index
· · · · · · ·

Index

Index

•••••••

Index

• • • • • •

235

Index

•••••••

Index

•••••••